PHILOSOPHY OF LITERATURE

'This is an intelligent, scrupulously fair-minded, closely argued treatment of central topics in the philosophy of literature. It will undoubtedly serve as a helpful introduction to this area for both philosophy and literature undergraduates.'

Professor Peter Lamarque, University of Hull

Literature is a discipline which poses its own characteristic philosophical questions. Literary theorists have been primarily engaged with discussions of the nature of literature, while 'analytic' philosophers have addressed literary problems within the framework of aesthetics, or in a manner which is accessible only to a philosophical audience. The present book redresses the balance by examining issues in the philosophy of literature from an analytic standpoint accessible to both students of literature and students of philosophy.

The book discusses definitions of literature, the distinction between oral and written literature and the identity of literary works. The author offers a wide-ranging discussion of the nature of fiction, in which both irony and non-literary fictions are analysed. An examination of our emotional involvement with fictional characters and events, followed by a discussion of the concept of imagination as an essential factor in our apprehension of literary works. Various theories of metaphor are then considered, and postmodernist theories of authorship discussed. Issues about truth and morality in literature are also raised. Finally, the book asks whether literary appraisals are objective or subjective and proposes a qualified subjective view.

The book presupposes no philosophical knowledge in the reader, is free of jargon and sets out problems and solutions in a clear and accessible way. At the same time, it offer fresh approaches to traditional problems and raises new issues in the philosophy of literature.

Christopher New is former Head of the Department of Philosophy at the University of Hong Kong. He is also the author of a number of novels.

PHILOSOPHY OF LITERATURE

An Introduction

Christopher New

London and New York

First published 1999
by Routledge

11 New Fetter Lane, London EC4P 4EE
Simultaneously published in the USA and Canada
by Routledge
29 West 35th Street, New York, NY 10001

© 1999 Christopher New

Typeset in Times by Routledge
Printed and bound in Great Britain by
Mackays of Chatham PLC, Kent

British Library Cataloguing in Publication Data
A catalogue record for this book is available from the British Library

Library of Congress Cataloging in Publication Data
New, Christopher.
Philosophy of literature: an introduction/Christopher New.
p.cm.
Includes bibliographical references and index.
1. Literature—Philosophy. I. Title.
PN45.N38 1998
801—DC21
98-39518
CIP

ISBN 0-415-14485-X (hbk)
ISBN 0-415-14486-8 (pbk)

CONTENTS

PREFACE

Although this is a book of philosophy, it is intended as much for those with literary as for those with philosophical interests, and I have therefore assumed no prior knowledge of philosophy in the reader. And although it is an introductory book, I have not hesitated to argue for my own views where I thought that other views, even widely accepted ones, were mistaken. I have generally discussed those other views in the text but, where space did not permit that, I have drawn attention to them in the notes.

The standpoint from which this book was written would probably be loosely described as analytic, which differentiates it from the many current theoretical works on literature which are written from a Deconstructionist or generally 'postmodernist' standpoint. I have not discussed postmodernist theories, but that does not imply I do not think them worth discussing. Indeed, I had originally intended to include a discussion of them in the book, and my eventual decision not to do so was based on pragmatic, not critical, grounds. I realised, as the work progressed, that to be of any value, a consideration of those theories would involve lengthy explanations and distracting argument, which would make the book unwieldy and frustrate its purpose as an introduction. This book, therefore, where it deals with topics which postmodernist theories also discuss, does not represent a dismissal of those theories, but an alternative to them.

The nature of philosophical argument tends to make disagreement more prominent than agreement, but that disagreement often occurs against a far wider, if less visible, background of agreement. So it is in this case. I disagree with some of the views of Kendall Walton and Gregory Currie, as well as with some of those advanced in the recent work of Peter Lamarque and Stein Haugom Olsen, and of Malcolm Budd. But I have learnt much from, and agree with much of, what they say. I am indebted to them in particular, as well as to the other writers mentioned in the text, for the various ways in which their thoughts have provoked and helped me clarify my own.

ACKNOWLEDGEMENTS

The author and publisher would like to thank copyright holders for giving their permission to reproduce extracts from the following copyright material:

Joyce Cary (1968) *Herself Surprised*, Caldar & Boyars, London. By permission of the trustees of the J.L.A. Cary Estate.

W.H.Davies (1943) *Collected Poems*, Jonathan Cape. By permission of the Executors of the W. H. Davies Estate.

T.S. Eliot (1923) 'The Function of Criticism', *Criterion*, October. By permission of Faber and Faber Ltd.

A.E. Housman (1939) *A Shropshire Lad*, Jonathan Cape, London. By permission of the Society of Authors as the literary representative of the Estate of A.E. Housman.

R.D.Laing (1970) *Knots*, Tavistock Publications.

Philip Larkin (1995) 'Places, Loved Ones' from *The Less Deceived*, Marvell Press. By permission of The Marvell Press, England and Australia.

S.H.Olsen, 'Literary Aesthetics, Literary Practice' in *Mind*, October 1981, pp. 521-41. By permission of Oxford University Press.

Amos Oz (1974) *Elsewhere, Perhaps*, Martin Secker & Warburg. By permission of Random House and Harcourt Brace & Co. Edition cited in text, Penguin 1979.

Dylan Thomas (1952) *Collected Poems*, J.M. Dent and Sons.

Every effort has been made to contact copyright holders. If we have inadvertently failed to acknowledge copyright, please contact the publisher.

1

WHAT IS LITERATURE? CLEARING THE GROUND

Prologue

Suppose you are reading Eliot's *The Waste Land*, Shakespeare's *King Lear*, Joyce's *Ulysses*, or Chekhov's *Ward Number Six*. What you are reading is a poem, a play, a novel, a short story. We would also say you are reading a work of literature, or of imaginative literature – though in the case of *King Lear*, some might be inclined to deny that, wishing to distinguish literature sharply from drama.

Now suppose you are reading the classical Athenian politician Demosthenes's *Philippics*, Sir Thomas Browne's *Urn Burial*, the Roman poet Lucretius's *On the Nature of Things*, or the Sermon on the Mount from the New Testament. What you are reading now is a work of oratory, an essay, philosophy or scripture. But, again, we would also say you are reading a work of literature – what you are reading is both a work of oratory, an essay, philosophy or scripture and a work of literature.

Suppose, finally, you are reading Frederick Forsyth's *Day of the Jackal*, the products of a Victorian poetaster, a story in *Just Seventeen*, or the Reverend C. T. Awdry's *George, the Big Engine*. What you are reading now is a novel, poetry (or verse), or stories. We might also say you are reading literature, but we would scarcely say it was serious literature – it is 'popular', or 'light', or 'children's' literature. Or some might say it was not ('was not really') literature at all. It is not good, or important, enough, they might say, to deserve the title of literature.

These are some of the things we must explain in trying to understand what literature is. Three things seem to stand out immediately: we may doubt whether drama is literature; a literary work need not be exclusively, or even primarily, a literary work; and we may use the term 'literature' and its cognates in either a neutral or an honorific way. I will say something about each of these points in turn.

The problem of drama

Why should we doubt whether drama is literature? One answer is that drama is a performing art, while literature is not. We do not perform novels or poetry, it may be said, while we do perform dances, plays and music. Hence drama must belong with the performing arts, not with literature.

This conclusion is too hasty. Why should not drama belong to both categories? Why should not some works of literature be performable? Indeed, we may wonder whether someone giving a reading of a novel (e.g. on the radio), or a public recital of some poetry, is not giving a performance just as much as actors are in acting a play. If they are, then novels and poetry are as performable as plays, although they may not 'require' to be performed in the way plays normally do.

Yet there are plays which clearly cannot be literature – mime plays, for instance. The reason why they are not literature indicates, unsurprisingly, not only the solution of the question of drama, but also something about the nature of literature itself. Literature is necessarily linguistic; it is distinguished from painting, sculpture, music, dance, architecture, etc., by its use of language. Language, that is words, is to the author roughly (only roughly) what paint is to the painter. The difference between the poet and the novelist on the one hand, and the dramatist on the other is that the poet and the novelist are restricted to language alone, while the dramatist is not. The poet and the novelist have nothing but language with which to depict character, action, feeling, thought, location, etc., whereas the dramatist can rely also on gesture, movement, and visual or sound effects. But that does not mean the dramatist's work cannot be classed as literature. It will count as literature to the extent that he, too, uses language as the nondramatist author does to depict character, thought, feeling, action, etc., and this is a matter of degree. At one extreme, there are mime plays, which are the works of mime artists, and dance dramas which are the works of choreographers, not playwrights. Since language has no part in these works, they are not classifiable as literature. We also have acted, but wordless, plays (not mimes), such as Samuel Beckett's *Breath*. At the other extreme, we have radio plays without sound effects, in which the whole work is done, as in a novel, by the author's use of language, and the actors' speaking of it; and these are works of (dramatic) literature. In between lie the majority of dramas, such as *King Lear*, in which language is used in conjunction with the resources of the stage; and in these plays, too, the author's use of language justifies us in calling them literary works. (That is why film scripts are rarely classifiable as literary works – in films language is almost invariably subordinate to the visual image.) Drama is thus a category that cuts across literature. To say that a work is literary is partly to say that it uses language. To say that it is drama is to say, among other things, that it standardly requires to be performed. But being a work that

2

requires to be performed does not prevent a play from being a work of literature as well.

But what do we mean by 'language'? We can speak of the language of music or films, the language of dance, the language of love, and body language. … If 'language' has so many meanings, it may seem, not much will be excluded, so not much will be being claimed when we say that literature is essentially linguistic. The sense of 'language' in which I make this claim, however, is a restricted one. 'Language', as I am using the term, refers to a lexicon, syntax and semantics, such as is exhibited by French, English, Russian, Chinese, etc. Music, films, dance, love and bodies do not have a language in that sense. There is no lexicon of love or syntax of body language as there is of Chinese and French. Nor is there a semantics of music. It is only language in the restricted sense that is essential to literature.

Uses of 'literature'

Having settled the doubt about drama, we can turn to the other two points that emerged from my brief survey of usage. These are more positive. The first was that literary works need not be exclusively literary works. A work on urn burial, philosophy or science may also be a work of literature, whether good or bad. We may agree or disagree with the speculations Sir Thomas Browne founds on the evidence of urn burial, and we may also enjoy or dislike the metaphors and cadences in which he presents those speculations. The first response expresses an archaeological, the second a literary, interest. It seems, moreover, that works which are not literary works at all may yet have literary qualities, good or bad. A philosophical argument may be expressed clumsily or elegantly, a text book may be vivid or dull, and even the minutes of a board meeting may be written in a way that is either crisp or soggy. We would not call these things literature, as we would call *Urn Burial* or *On the Nature of Things* literature; and if we ask why not, we raise the second positive point that emerged from our survey of usage. For the answer seems to be either that their literary qualities play a minor role in the whole work, and therefore they are not classifiable as literature, whether good or bad; or else their literary qualities are poor and unremarkable, and therefore they do not deserve the honorific title of (good) literature.

In the one answer, we are classifying works neutrally, by the size of the role that literary qualities play in the whole work, whether those works exhibit good or bad instances of such qualities; in the other answer, we seem to be classifying works only according to the value of their literary qualities. And the second positive point was just that literature and its cognates may be used in a neutral or an honorific way. When we contrast literature with science or history, or contrast serious literature with escapist literature, we are using the word 'literature' in a neutral, value-free way. If we say of a *Just Seventeen* story that it is not literature, we are using the word in an honorific way – the story, we imply, simply lacks literary *value*, and for that reason should not have the title of literature conferred upon it. The cognate phrases 'work of literature' and 'literary work' function in the same way. If asked to place all the books on a desk into two piles, one labelled 'literary works', or 'works of literature', and the second labelled 'other works', we might put books we regard as worthless fiction onto the first pile, along with *Anna Karenina* (taking 'literary works' in a neutral way), or we might put them onto the second pile (taking it in an honorific way). In neither case would we be wrong; we would merely be classifying according to the different principles which the flexibility of the expression permits. That is why a crisp agenda for a board meeting, if a copy were on the desk, would normally be placed on the pile labelled 'other works'. For by neither principle would it normally be classified as literature; its nonliterary qualities as a business document play a far more prominent part in the whole than its sole literary quality of crispness; so that prevents it from being classified as literature according to the neutral sense of the word. Its sole quality of crispness has only mild literary value; so it does not count as literature in the honorific sense, either.

These last points suggest we can define 'literature' in two ways, corresponding to the neutral and the honorific uses of the word. We can define it, we may think, either as writings that have a certain neutral property, or properties, 'literariness'; or as writings that have a high degree of a certain type of value, 'literary value'. This could only be a first step of course, for until we eliminated the words 'literariness' and 'literary value' from them, the definitions would be circular. So the next step, apparently, would be to establish which features of writings confer literariness, and which confer literary value upon them.

A double programme thus seems, dauntingly, to present itself. However, I intend to follow only one of them, the easier one of establishing what it is that makes a work a literary work. The second question, what makes a literary work a good one, is a question I shall not discuss here. Of course, the answer to that question is provided in an empty way by the answer to the first one: what makes it a literary work at all? For if literary works are works with certain properties, then good literary works will be those with good instances of those properties, just as, if metaphysical books are inquiries into the nature of things, then good metaphysical books will be those which are good instances of inquiries into the nature of things. But that does not tell us what counts as a good or bad instance. Although I shall not discuss that question explicitly here, I shall give reasons in Chapter 9 for thinking there is a subjective element in literary appraisals and that the goodness of literary works therefore lies partly in the mind of the beholder.

Leaving the question of literary value on one side for the present, then we might think we ought to start the search for literariness now; but we need to settle a preliminary issue first, an issue which may have occurred to some readers already. The issue is this: I have been speaking of literature and the definition of literature, in terms of writings, and all the examples I have given so far have been of written works. But this way of speaking is inaccurate, the examples misleading. For many literary works are not written at all; they are oral works. It might seem a simple matter to resolve this issue. All we have to do, we might think, is replace the word 'writings' with some such phrase as 'written or oral works' and it is true, that would remedy the inaccuracy. But it would tell us nothing of the role of writing in literature, or of the complex and interesting relations of the written and the spoken word. These relations deserve to be explored a little, not least because they rarely are. I shall therefore delay examining the idea of literariness until I have said something about them. This in turn will lead to a discussion of the identity criteria of literary works, from which we shall return eventually to the question of literariness.

Oral and written literature

What has writing to do with literature? Since many literary works were composed, and hence existed, before they were written down (and some never have been written down, and never will be), it is clearly wrong, despite the etymology of the word, to define literature as we did just now, and as the dictionary does, in terms of writings alone. Literature may exist in either written or oral form. Indeed, all the earliest literature existed only in oral form; the market place storyteller, the ancestor of today's novelist, recited oral, not written, stories. This point, once stated, seems numbingly obvious and we may wonder, therefore, why we nevertheless speak as if it were not even true, never mind obvious; as if, that is, literature consisted entirely of written works.

The answer, I suspect, is twofold. First, the great bulk of extant, and especially of sophisticated, literature, whether originally oral or not, is now in written form; it is this that meets the eye, especially, perhaps the scholar's eye. Second, we tend to suppose, perhaps, that whereas all oral literature could exist in written form (as most surviving literature that was originally oral does now), not all written literature could exist in oral form. This second reason deserves a closer look. There seem to be two claims involved in it, one of causal, the other of logical, impossibility: one, that long and complex works such as, say, Proust's twelve volume *Remembrance of Things Past*, could not have been composed in unwritten form, since they exceed the mind's ability to compose, revise and edit with the resources of memory alone; the other is that some written works exploit features peculiar to written language, and consequently could not have been composed or subsequently exist exactly the same in unwritten form.

The first claim is hard to settle conclusively. On the one hand, the human mind is capable of prodigious achievements, but there are surely limits to what it can do unaided; and if these are not transgressed in Proust's work, there must be possible works which would transgress them. (I am not thinking here of unfinished works of infinite length, but simply of very long completed works.) On the other hand, no oral work can be too long or complex to have been originally composed in written form or be subsequently written down. However, the deficiencies of our memories could well have been made good by the use of such technologically advanced extensions to them as tape recorders rather than by writing. And while it is hard to see how the considerable body of theory and instructions for its application, upon which the invention of recording devices depends, could possibly have existed without the prior invention of writing – particularly when we include the writing of numerals and the construction of wiring diagrams – this is irrelevant. For 'literature' might still have been an oral phenomenon. There seems no particular reason to think that any written work is so long or complex that it could not have been composed orally.

If the first claim is contestable, though, the second is not. Works that make use of certain resources of written language cannot exist unchanged in oral form. We must think here, of course, only of the resources that are peculiar to written language. It would be wrong to cite the use of bold type, for instance where that is simply the written counterpart of oral emphasis, just as the question mark is the written counterpart of a questioning intonation in speech. The cases we should consider are, rather, the use of italics to indicate introspection or a change of time; of the symbolic layout of some metaphysical religious poetry (the altar poems of Herbert, the cruciform verses of Traherne or the diamond shapes that Dylan Thomas sometimes uses); of the deliberate use of lower case letters as in ee cummings's verse and much contemporary poetry; of acronyms and eye rhymes. These devices may sometimes be trivial, but they are still features of literary works, and they have no oral counterparts; they are logically dependent on writing. The literary works employing them have therefore an indispensably written, or graphic, dimension. They could neither be composed nor exist intact in oral form, whereas all oral literature could have been composed and could exist in written form.

These facts may explain why we are tempted to think of literature in terms of writing, but they cannot, of course, justify us in succumbing to the temptation. All that they tell us is that some works of literature (not all works) could not have existed as they do if writing had not been invented. It is salutary to recall that the role played by writing in literary composition is often one that could as well be, and sometimes is, played by a tape-recorder. The poet often composes his verses orally before he writes them down line by line, referring to those he has already composed and written down, as he might equally well have referred to his recorded voice. Prose writers often do the same. Writing functions here simply as a means of recording, not as an element in the work itself – it is comparatively few works that have an indispensably graphic dimension. Hence the composition of long and complex works depends on writing only secondarily; an extension to our memory is what is primarily required, and it is that which the invention of writing facilitates.

What I have just said may give the impression that it is mere coincidence that many literary works are composed in oral stages which are then written down. But that would be a mistake. They are composed orally because they are destined for an audience in the original meaning of that term (people who hear). They are to be heard, as well as read; and it is only to be expected that the author should want to hear them himself as he composes.

It is true that some written works exploit the peculiar qualities of written language. It follows from this, of course, not only that they could not have been composed entirely orally, but also that they could not be fully appreciated if they were only heard and never read; a purely auditory apprehension of those works must leave something out. But it is equally true that in many of those works, and in a host of others, there is also an indispensably auditory dimension. They cannot be fully appreciated if they are only read, and never heard. Just as some literature exploits the written, so most exploits the spoken, word. We noticed, discussing drama, that poetry can be recited in a public performance. Whether it is heard in private or in public, all poetry is meant to be heard, even if some is also meant to be seen, but much prose also requires to be read aloud in order to be fully appreciated. We have only to think of the King James version of The Bible or Sir Thomas Browne's writings to be convinced of this, and even in prose works that do not need to be heard in their entirety there are often passages which are not fully appreciated if they are not spoken.

Of course, there are many prose works in which the auditory element is comparatively insignificant, and which not only do not require, but may even require not, to be heard in their entirety. It is possible that the proportion of such works is increasing, for it is hard to find a modern analogue of Sir Thomas Browne. (There is, no doubt, a sociological explanation for this; we read silently more quickly than we read aloud, and we have less time to read than most people who read used to have.) But for all poetry and much prose, it is still true that it must be heard in order to be fully appreciated. For these works, the written word exists not merely to be read silently as we may read an advertisement in the newspaper, but also to be heard, whether aloud, *sotto voce*, or in the reader's imagination. (It is worth remembering how recently it is that people gave up reading aloud to others, as characters do in Jane Austen's fictional drawing rooms – a decline that the advent of the audio tape may be starting to reverse.) The role of writing here is like, though not exactly like, the role of the score in music; the written word, like the musical notation, requires to be translated into sound.

The likeness, I said, is not exact; and we should not be misled by it, for the score and the written word are importantly different. Musical notation has no other function than to represent sounds, or qualities of and relations between sounds, whereas the written sentences of literature that require to be read or spoken aloud (and, of course, written sentences in general) standardly have the additional quality of being meaningful – a quality they possess whether they are read in silence or aloud. The reading of a musical score is in this sense a merely auditory affair – we either imagine the sounds represented in it, or directly produce them – while the reading of a literary or any other written work is not. Music, we noted earlier, does not have a semantic dimension in the way that literature does.

There are a few literary works with an indispensable graphic dimension, many with an indispensable auditory dimension, and some with neither. Works with an indispensable auditory dimension require to be heard, however they were composed; works with an indispensable graphic dimension may require to be both heard and read. But to return to the definition of literature, literary works are to be defined, if at all, in terms neither of written nor of oral, but of linguistic composition – a conclusion obvious enough, once it is drawn, and one already foreshadowed in our investigation of the status of drama. We could have literature without writing, and we could even have literature without speech; but we could not have literature without language.

Compositions and their forms: copies and originals

We have now answered the questions raised by the existence of oral as well as written literature. But before examining definitions of literariness, we should consider one more question that arises out of what we have just been saying, for not everything is clear here. The same composition can exist in written and in oral form; but what is the relation of the composition itself to the oral and the written forms, which one, if any, is the composition? This question involves another. The same composition can be spoken and recorded, copied and printed, any number of times. What is the relation of the repeated recitations and recordings, or of the printed copies, to the composition of which they are recitations, recordings or copies? These questions extend beyond literature; they arise for any linguistic composition. A political speech and a cooking recipe, for instance, can exist in written or oral form, and can be copied or recorded just as easily as a poem, and the questions that arise for a poem will, therefore, also arise about the speech or recipe – What is the relation of the recipe or speech to the sounds or inscriptions made in producing it, and what is its relation to its copies or recordings? As the questions are so general we can discuss them initially in terms of some nonliterary and simple examples; their very plainness will prevent us from being distracted by the irrelevant qualities that literary examples might also afford.

First, whenever we write or speak, whenever we produce a linguistic composition, however slight, we utter sequences of written marks (inscriptions) or sounds. (For reasons of economy, not disrespect, I shall ignore here nonvocal, nonwritten languages, such as the American Sign Language. My remarks can, however, be easily adjusted to accommodate them.) These inscriptions or sounds have, as well as other features, certain grammatical and semantic ones that are determined by the rules of the language which we speak or write. These rules determine both how the sequences of sounds or inscriptions constitute words and sentences, and what the sentences mean. (There is a large and pitfall-ridden field of theory on how exactly these sequences get a meaning. As our interest is not in that question – we are presupposing that somehow they do – I shall not venture into it.) The rules also determine (together with certain intentions of the utterer) what statements, questions, orders, etc. we issue when we utter the sentences that are constituted by those sequences of sounds or inscriptions that we speak or write. Thus, whether the sentence 'I will pay you five dollars' is a promise or merely a prediction depends both on the rules of English and on the intentions of the speaker. (We shall return to this topic in more detail in Chapter 2, when discussing the 'speech act' definition of 'imaginative literature'.)

Concatenations of sentences in which statements, questions, orders, etc. are issued form what is sometimes called a discourse. Occasionally, in the limiting case, when by rather obscure criteria, the statement, question, etc. is considered to be both important enough and complete, single sentences may form a discourse. More often they do so only in large numbers, when they are connected by the fairly clear relation of identity of authorship and the fairly murky relation of identity of topic, and when, again, they are considered important enough and complete. Simonides's brief epitaph on the Spartans who died at Thermopylae is a one-sentence discourse:

> Go stranger, tell the Lacedaemonians
> that here, obeying their commands, we lie.[1]

Aeschylus's tragedy *The Persian Women*, written a little later, is a discourse consisting of many sentences. An anthology of poetry is not a discourse, although it contains many discourses. Nor is an encyclopedia or a telephone directory. But poems, political tracts, novels, scientific treatises and parliamentary speeches are all discourses.

What is the relation of the discourse to the sequences of sounds or inscriptions in issuing which we produce our discourses? Is the discourse just those sounds or inscriptions? Or is it both those and the indefinitely many copies that may be made of it in recordings or printings? Or is it neither of these? The question, I remarked, does not concern discourses alone. 'Discourse' is a term we reserve for the grander products of our linguistic endeavours, but exactly the same puzzle arises for the fruits of our humbler efforts as well. If anyone writes or says the words 'Cats eat fish', and thereby states that cats eat fish (i.e. is not merely practising English pronunciation, talking in his sleep, etc., but expressing his belief), the question arises at once, and in the same way as for *Anna Karenina*, of the relation of his statement to the sequence of sounds or inscriptions in uttering which he made it. Just as there is a related question for *Anna Karenina* of the relation of the novel to the many thousands of copies or recordings that are made of it, so there is a related question for the statement of its relation to the many copies or recordings that could, but probably will not, be made of it.

Let us discuss the supposed statement *Cats eat fish* first. Not that there are not important differences between them. *Anna Karenina* is a novel, a work of fiction, whereas *Cats eat fish* is a simple statement of fact; and the one is a much more complex thing than the other. In considering the sentence *Cats eat fish* as a statement, for instance, we assess it solely in terms of truth and falsity. But in considering *Anna Karenina* as a novel, we do not assess it – or certainly not directly, or solely – in terms of truth and falsity; a whole gamut of dimensions is brought in with the novel which are inappropriate to the consideration of utterances merely as statements. But these differences are not relevant now, for both are alike in that they are issued in words spoken or written, and (let us suppose) subsequently repeated, in sequences of sounds or inscriptions. It is only the relation of the thing in each case – of the nonfiction statement or the set of (mainly) fictional utterances – to its sequences of sounds or inscriptions that concerns us now. The further, distinctive, characteristics of fictional, and other literary, works are irrelevant to this concern.

Is the statement *Cats eat fish* just the particular sequence of sounds or inscriptions ('Cats eat fish') uttered at a certain time by a certain speaker or writer? Surely not; for that particular sequence may have been made in a wavering tenor voice or printed large in red ink; and the quality of the voice or the size and colour of the ink, like many other features of the sounds or inscriptions, are clearly no part of the statement made when the sequence 'Cats eat fish' is uttered. Besides, the sounds are evanescent, and the inscriptions can be erased, yet the statement made in uttering them can be considered long after that particular sequence of sounds or inscriptions has ceased to exist – and considered, too, by people who never heard or read that sequence.

What this suggestion fails to recognise is that the statement, and the sentence in uttering which it is made, are not identical with, but an abstraction from, those sounds and inscriptions. We noticed just now that the sounds and inscriptions we produce when we speak or write have certain grammatical and semantic features that are determined by the rules of the language we are speaking or writing. These rules confer on the raw sounds or marks we make the characteristic of grammaticality and meaning; they make them utterances of sentences, and in the appropriate circumstances, issuings of statements. When we speak and write, we produce sounds and inscriptions, certainly; but it is only certain features of those sounds and inscriptions that are grammatically and semantically relevant; the others can be ignored. It is for this reason that both the sentence and the statement may be called an abstraction from the sounds and inscriptions uttered in making them. It is for this reason, too, that a statement can be made indifferently either in speech or in writing. Ink marks have few physical characteristics in common with sounds. But they both have the same grammatical and semantic features by conforming to the same linguistic rules, rather as two different types of material can both realise the same design. It is by virtue of their possessing the same grammatical and semantic features that uttering these two quite different sequences can constitute making the same statement.

We should, then, amend the suggestion I have just rejected. The statement, we should say, is the sentence that is abstracted from the whole sequence of sounds and inscriptions which the author utters. In uttering the sounds and inscriptions that he does, the author also utters words which constitute a sentence and have meaning. In seriously uttering that sentence with that meaning, he makes a statement; the statement is just that sentence which he utters in making the sounds or inscriptions that he does. (This is oversimplified; it will get refined shortly.) The relation of the sentence which constitutes the statement to the sounds or inscriptions he utters is thus analogous to the relation of a move in chess to the physical motions performed in making it. You can move a piece across the board without making a move in the game, just as you can utter the sequence 'Cats eat fish' without making a statement; in both cases, for instance, you may be pretending or demonstrating. There are many features of the physical movements involved in moving a piece in chess which are irrelevant, such as whether one lifts the piece two or four inches above the board, with which hand one lifts it, or which part of the piece one holds. Similarly, there are many features of the sounds or marks one utters in making a statement that are equally irrelevant, such as the timbre or volume of the voice, the style of the handwriting, the colour of the ink or the size of the type face. What constitutes the sequence of motions as a move in chess is the rules of the game, just as what constitutes the sequence of sounds or inscriptions as a statement is the rules of the language. Finally, making a move in chess is not something over and above performing the motions involved in lifting the piece and putting it down; it is performing that sequence of movements in a way that conforms to the rules of chess. Similarly, making a statement is not something over and above uttering a sequence of sounds or inscriptions; it is uttering that sequence of sounds or inscriptions in a way that conforms to the rules of the language.

There is a plausible objection that might be made here. It is that the suggestion just made is no real improvement on the suggestion it is supposed to amend. For to say that the statement is the sentence which is 'abstracted' from the total sequence of sounds or inscriptions uttered seems to be no more than to say that we disregard those features of the sounds and inscriptions that are not grammatically and semantically relevant. That surely leaves us with the other features of the same (evanescent) sounds or (erasable) inscriptions that are relevant – what is abstracted is just as evanescent or erasable as what it is abstracted from. The reason for rejecting the previous suggestion was that we can consider someone's statement without considering any part of the actual sequence of sounds or inscriptions which they uttered in making the statement – a sequence which may well have disappeared by the time we come to consider the statement. But the amendment is as vulnerable to that objection as the original suggestion was. For in both cases we have perishable goods – physical sounds or inscriptions – which do or may not survive the occasion of their production

The answer to this objection (and the refinement of the oversimplification of two paragraphs back) is that what we consider in cases where the original sequence of sounds or inscriptions is no longer available is another sequence, the grammatical and semantic features of which are the same as those of the sequence that has now disappeared (or relevantly similar to them – the need for this qualification, which it would be tedious to repeat every time I speak of identity, will become clear shortly). We hear, read or think of a different sequence of sounds or inscriptions, but that different sequence, by virtue of the identity of its grammatical and semantic features with those of the original, constitutes an utterance of the same sentence, the making of the same statement. For there is no relevant grammatical or semantic difference between the two sequences. So the sentence is not, after all, evanescent or erasable in the way the sequences of sounds or inscriptions in which it is uttered are. It is like a pattern made with matches. If the matches are lit and burnt up, *they* cannot be used to make the same pattern, but the same pattern can be made with *other* matches; in considering the pattern made with those other matches, we are considering different matches, but the same pattern.

This answer provides us also with the solution to the problem of the relation of the statement to the copies that can be made of it. The making of the statement *Cats eat fish* is a unique event which occurs when a particular person utters the sequence of sounds or inscriptions (e.g. the English sentence 'Cats eat fish') in which, through conformity to the rules of the language, the statement is issued. The statement is the sentence which is uttered on that occasion. But the utterance of other sequences of sounds or inscriptions, with all their various qualities of volume or pitch, colour or type size, will be utterances of the same sentence, hence the making of the same statement, in so far as those other sequences, despite their differences from each other, and from the original sequence, all have the same grammatical and semantic features. The sentence is uttered, and the statement issued, we may say, in any uttering of a sequence of sounds or inscriptions that has just those grammatical and semantic features.

On the one hand, different people independently, or the same person on different occasions, may make the same statement, *Cats eat fish*, by different utterings of sequences of sounds or inscriptions which all have the same grammatical and semantic features. On the other hand, and this is what concerns us now, copies of the statement may be made in written, electronic, or some other form, and then each of those copies will be an uttering of the (same) sentence, an issuing of the (same) statement. The only difference between these copies and the first sequence in which the statement was made is that the sequence of sounds and inscriptions which are uttered subsequently are not original, but derivative. They are uttered, that is, as having the same grammatical and semantic features that the sequences of sounds or inscriptions uttered by the original author had, as being, therefore, the sentence then uttered, the statement then made. We may thus speak of each of these separate, derived sequences (in so far as they have the same grammatical and semantic features) indifferently either as copies of the author's statement or simply as the author's statement. To speak of them as copies is to draw attention to their causal dependence on the first. To speak of them as the author's statement is to proclaim the irrelevance of that dependence for purposes of identifying that statement. For the statement is the sentence uttered in any sequence of sounds or inscriptions that has just those grammatical and semantic features which the original sequence had. (This, too, is a simplification, though not an oversimplification, which will be refined later.) That is how it is possible for different people in different parts of the world to consider the same statement while inspecting a different sequence of inscriptions or hearing a different sequence of sounds. They inspect or hear different sequences, but they read or hear the same sentence, the same statement. To put it with a certain paradoxical succinctness: copies of statements are the same statements as the statements they are copies of.

I have been using a very simple case of stating as a model, and I have deliberately left out complications, such as those posed by statements in which 'indexical' terms, like 'I', 'you', 'now', 'then', 'here' or 'there' are used. These terms serve, again through the rules of the language, to link the sequence of sounds or inscriptions to some feature of the utterance context – the time, the place, the person, etc. (That is why they are called 'indexicals': they 'point' to one of those features.) Thus the same sequence of sounds or inscriptions, if it contained indexicals, would not always yield the same statement: 'Queen Elizabeth has just gone to Windsor' uttered in 1997 would not make the same statement as the same sentence uttered in 1594, despite being the same sequence of sounds or inscriptions, because the proper name and the adverb in it would refer to different people and times on each occasion of their utterance. The rules of indexicality in language are what make these differences possible; but I am not going to say how they do so. Some intricacy of argument is required for these cases, but they would leave the solution to our present problems unaffected; so there is no need to pick our way through the labyrinthine details of indexicality-explication.

I have not said anything yet about another complication, either: our ability to make or consider the 'same statement' in different languages. We can handle this complication by saying, briefly, that the sentences we regard as translations in other languages of the English sentence 'Cats eat fish', which clearly are quite different sequences of sounds or inscriptions with, possibly, quite different grammatical and semantic features, can be regarded as 'corresponding' sentences in those languages. Identity of statement across languages is thus secured, in so far as it is secured, not by identity of the sound or inscription sequences, nor by identity of grammatical and semantic features, but by a correspondence between different grammatical and semantic systems. A similar account can be given for translation within a language, when two different sentences ('Cats eat fish' and 'Cats are piscivorous', for instance) are regarded as being synonymous, as constituting the same statement.[2]

Application to literature

Though this account is simplified, and developed solely in terms of stating, the answers it provides will apply not only to mundane statements, questions, orders, etc., which we would scarcely dignify with the title of discourses, but also to those linguistic compositions that we would unhesitatingly classify as discourses, whether literary or not. Lincoln's *Gettysburg Address*, for example, is a discourse consisting of the concatenation of sentences which President Lincoln uttered in making the inscriptions or sound sequences that he did in November 1863. It was delivered in the sequence of sounds that he uttered shortly after the battle of Gettysburg. Other sequences of sounds (live or recorded) or inscriptions that constitute the same concatenation of sentences and are derived from Lincoln's are to be called indifferently either his *Address* or readings or copies of his *Address*. To hear a reading of the *Address* is to hear the *Address*, just as to read a copy of it is to read it. It is true, of course, that we might admire the *Address*, but dislike a particular reading of it, even Lincoln's. But that does not show, as may sometimes be confusedly supposed, that in hearing a reading of the *Address* we are not really hearing the *Address*. A reading of the *Address* is indeed a different thing from the *Address*, just as making a move in chess is a different thing from the move one makes. But one cannot listen to a reading of the *Address* without listening to the *Address*, any more than one can watch someone making a move in chess without watching the move. If we admire the *Address*, but dislike a reading of it, what we admire are the statements, pleas, exhortations, etc. that Lincoln uttered, and the balance, phrasing, rhythm, imagery, etc. of his sentences; what we dislike are the voice or manner in which those sentences are spoken. But so long as the sentences are indeed those, or copies of those, that Lincoln uttered, we are listening to his *Address*.

In the same way, *Anna Karenina* is the discourse consisting of the concatenation of (mainly) Russian sentences uttered by Tolstoy in the writing of a certain sequence of inscriptions which was completed, or at any rate published, in 1875–77.[3] Other sequences of inscriptions (or sounds) with the same grammatical and semantic features, which are thus the same concatenation of sentences, are to be called indifferently either *Anna Karenina* also, or copies of *Anna Karenina* – as are the concatenations of corresponding sentences in other languages, uttered in wholly different sequences of inscriptions (or sounds) which are accepted as translations of the concatenations of sentences first uttered by Tolstoy. Readings, live or recorded, of *Anna Karenina* are given by utterings of Tolstoy's sentences (or the corresponding sentences in other languages) in the form of sequences of sounds; and those spoken concatenations of sentences are to be called indifferently either *Anna Karenina* or readings, or recordings, of *Anna Karenina*; to hear a reading or recording of *Anna Karenina* is to hear *Anna Karenina*.

Finally, *King Lear* is the concatenation of sentences uttered in the inscriptions or sounds made by Shakespeare, or any copy of that concatenation; that is, any derivative sequence of inscriptions or sounds with the same grammatical and semantic features that the sequence inscribed by Shakespeare possessed. Performances of *King Lear* involve spoken utterings of the same sentences by actors acting on the stage. Any performance, in so far as the actors utter in sequences of sounds the sentences uttered by Shakespeare in sequences of inscriptions, is *King Lear*. To watch a performance of *King Lear* is to watch *King Lear*, just as to hear a reading of *Anna Karenina* is to hear *Anna Karenina*. There is, of course, the difference that *Anna Karenina*, like most novels, may not require to be read aloud in order to be fully appreciated, whereas *King Lear*, like most plays, does require to be performed to be fully appreciated; and since it is poetry as well as drama, it is less incompletely appreciated when read aloud than when read silently. (Very much the same is true, of course, of Lincoln's *Gettysburg Address*, it is fully appreciated only when it is heard.) However, the play is just that concatenation of sentences which Shakespeare uttered in making the inscriptions that he did; and whether that concatenation is read silently, read aloud, or declaimed in the course of a stage (or film) production are questions about what is done with the play, not what the play is. (There are obvious, but limited, analogies here with the composer's holograph, the printed score, and the performance of the musical work.)

We have just touched upon one of the differences between prosaic statements such as *Cats eat fish* and literary discourses. It does not normally matter, for such a statement, whether it is by hearing or by reading it that you apprehend the sentence in which it is issued, whereas for many literary discourses, as we have seen, it may matter a great deal Moreover, in considering sentences strictly as statements, questions, orders, etc., it is inappropriate to consider how they sound, while in considering them as literature, hence in considering any literary discourse, that is never inappropriate; although how they sound may not (as with *Anna Karenina*) be the dominant, or sometimes (as with *The Day of the Jackal* perhaps) even an important, consideration.

A second, but frequently minor, difference is that it is sometimes appropriate to consider how the sentences look when thinking of them as literature, while that is never a consideration when thinking of them solely as statements, questions instructions, etc. Some literature has, as we noticed earlier, an ineliminable, if small, graphic dimension. (Recall such things as altar-, cross- and diamond-shaped poetry, eye-rhymes and ee cummings's verse.) Simple nonliterary statements do not have this feature.

A third difference, related to those already mentioned, is that grammar and semantics are relatively more rigid in literary discourses. By this I mean that whereas some grammatical and semantic variations may not affect the statement-function of a sentence, they will be much more likely – in some cases certain – to affect its literary qualities. An utterance of the sentence 'Cats are piscivorous' may well be accepted as making the same statement as an utterance of the sentence 'Cats eat fish' if we are satisfied that for the purposes in hand 'piscivorous' is synonymous with 'eat fish'; an utterance of 'Homeward plods the ploughman' may be regarded as making the same statement as an utterance of 'The ploughman plods homeward', if we are satisfied that for the purposes in hand the rearrangement makes no significant difference. This, indeed, is the reason for the qualification I made earlier, when discussing the identity of statements. The grammatical and semantic features of different sequences of sounds and inscriptions, I suggested, had to be the same, or 'relevantly similar', to establish identity. The reason for this qualification is that it would be too strict to demand exact identity of grammatical and semantic features. We need to relax our criteria so as to be able to allow for printer's errors, slips of the tongue or pen, misspellings and other minor deviations, as well as for the kind of rephrasing given above. These variations yield sentences which are different from the original sentences, but which may yet be relevantly similar to them, and so pass as constituting the same statement. Not that we will always let them pass; in some cases, such as legal documents, we may prefer to keep our criteria tight. But often we will.

The same holds, but generally less so, for literature. Some relaxation of criteria is allowable in literary discourses too, but the amount we can tolerate is much less; grammar and semantics are more rigid in them than in most other discourses. Thus the variation offered of the two sentences above would certainly matter when we considered them in terms of their literary qualities. The substitution of the rare and orotund Latin 'piscivorous' for the pithy Anglo-Saxon 'eat fish', and the consequent differences in suggestiveness and rhythm, in the first sentence, and the difference of emphasis, and, again, of suggestiveness and rhythm entailed by the relocation of 'Homeward plods' in the second, would certainly affect our appreciation of the two sentences from a literary point of view. The grammatical and semantic rigidity of sentences considered from that point of view is generally much greater than it is for sentences considered from other points of view. That, of course, is why literary discourses tend to be much more resistant to translation than nonliterary discourses, and the more resistant the more prominent are the features of the 'home' discourse which have no counterpart in other languages. We may accept a translation of the *Gettysburg Address* and a translation of *Anna Karenina* as being the *Gettysburg Address* and *Anna Karenina*. But we may well hesitate at a translation of *King Lear* and baulk at one of Pindar's *Odes*, preferring to call them translations, or versions, of *King Lear* and Pindar's *Odes*.

There is one more difference we should note, one that may already have aroused some qualms. It is that in the case of fiction, the author does not characteristically issue statements, questions, orders, etc. to his audience in uttering the sentences that he does; whereas in other discourses he does. Lincoln states 'The world will little note nor long remember what we say here, but it can never forget what they did here', and the schoolteacher states that 'cats eat fish'. But Shakespeare does not state in *The Merchant of Venice* that the quality of mercy is not strained; he creates a character, Portia, who states it. We may, perhaps, say that Shakespeare's character 'fictionally' states it, and we may believe that Shakespeare implies that what Portia fictionally states is actually true. But we cannot say that Shakespeare actually states it. Nor does Shakespeare inquire if it is a dagger that he sees before him; he creates a character, Macbeth, who 'fictionally' poses the question. But if that is so, we may wonder whether an account of the identity of linguistic compositions which is developed for statements, etc. can be applied directly to fictional contexts where there are not any statements, etc.

On reflection, though, we should see that this is no objection at all. Statements etc. were defined earlier as sentences uttered under certain conditions, and the identity of statements, etc. was defined in terms of the (tight or loose) identity of those sentences. Fictional statements etc. are not, indeed, genuine statements, etc., but they are concatenations of sentences, all the same. The identity of a novel, story or play is established through the identity of those sentences just as the identity of a statement, etc. is established through the identity of the sentences in which the statement is made – although, as we have seen, the criteria for sentence identity are generally much tighter in fictional, and all literary, sentences than they are in most nonliterary discourses. Both fictional and nonfictional sentences are the same kind of thing, differing only in the functions they are used to perform.

Conclusion

It is time to return to the proposed definition of literature, which we were about to explore before this rather lengthy digression. The definition was essentially this: Literature is writing that has a certain property, or certain properties, of literariness. The consequence of the digression is that we can now substitute 'linguistic composition' for 'writing'. This may not seem much of a profit, considering the outlay of intellectual labour – but only so long as we forget the invisible earnings that accrue from understanding the relation of written to oral literature and the status and identity-criteria of linguistic, especially literary, compositions.

2

WHAT IS LITERATURE? DEFINITIONS AND RESEMBLANCES

Prologue

The task would now seem to be to say what property or properties constitute literariness, what it is about a linguistic composition that makes it a literary one, whether good or bad. (I shall from now on use the word 'literary' only in the neutral sense, unless I indicate otherwise.) This way of formulating the question may suggest that there must be some property or properties such that if a work has them, it is a literary work, and if it is a literary work, it has them – that is, that there are necessary and sufficient conditions for the application of the term 'literary discourse', that literariness has an essence, fully present in every instance of literature, which can be captured in some verbal formula. This is how definitions have traditionally been conceived, and most theorists who have attempted to say what literature is, assuming such a traditional definition must be what they were after, have then set about looking for the formula, sometimes with a mounting sense of desperation.[1]

There is a difficulty about this project, however, that should make us pause. The difficulty is that the assumption may be false. Perhaps there is no essence. Perhaps what makes Tolstoy's *Anna Karenina* a literary discourse is not exactly the same as what makes Lucretius's *On the Nature of Things* one; and perhaps that in turn is not exactly what makes Shakespeare's *King Lear* or Donne's *Sermons* or Tennyson's *In Memoriam* one; and so on, through the whole range of literary discourses.

That would not mean that 'literary' was applied to these discourses merely homonymously, as 'pen' is applied homonymously to a writing instrument, a cattle enclosure and a female swan – three things that have nothing whatsoever in common by virtue of which the term is applied to them. For, though there would be no single property common to all literary discourses, by virtue of which they were literary discourses, there might be certain properties which some shared with others, while those others had additional properties which they in turn shared with yet other literary discourses ... Thus all literary discourses would resemble some other literary

19

discourses in some way, but they would not all resemble each other in a single way. It would be because of those various overlapping and criss-crossing resemblances that they would all be literary discourses.

Wittgenstein, the author of this account of how some words come to be applied in the way they are (although he did not speak of literature), charac-terised such overlapping resemblances as 'family resemblances', and words to which the account applies as family resemblance words.[2] The characteri-sation is apt, for the resemblances between different members of a family may overlap and criss-cross in the same way: the son may have the father's nose and complexion, but the mother's eyes; the daughter may have the father's eyes and nose, but the mother's complexion; the grandson may have the father's complexion, but the mother's eyes and nose. ... Thus, though each member of the family resembles some other member in some feature, they do not all resemble each other in just one feature or set of features. May it not be that literary discourses have a family resemblance in the same way, that the expression 'literary discourse' is a family resemblance expres-sion? If so, the search for what is common to all literary discourses will be fruitless at best. At worst, if we take a feature to be an essential one when it is not, it may end in distortion.

We should not assume, then, that 'literary discourse' must be defined in terms of necessary and sufficient conditions, that literature has an essence. But nor should we assume that the expression is a family resemblance term. What sort of expression it is cannot always be told in advance. The correct procedure therefore seems to be to survey the kinds of discourse that we call literary and see whether they in fact have some common property or proper-ties or, rather, exhibit a network of overlapping and criss-crossing resemblances. As Wittgenstein himself said on this very matter, we should not think, but look.[3]

The marginal cases problem

The procedure seems to be to survey the kinds of discourses that we call literary. But to do that, we must know what they are. We cannot discover what, if anything, is common to all of them, or which family resemblances they share, if we cannot initially distinguish between discourses that are literary and discourses which are not. It is here that another difficulty arises. Surely there are cases where we are not sure? We know that dramatic works such as *King Lear* are literary discourses, but what about works such as Plato's philosophical dialogue, *The Symposium*? We know that works of mathematical philosophy such as Russell and Whitehead's *Principia Mathematica* are not literary discourses, but what about biographical works like Lytton Strachey's *Eminent Victorians*? If we are not sure whether or not to count some works as literary discourses, it may seem as though we cannot even get started. For if we say that they are, we may find one thing common to all (supposed) literary discourses, or one set of family resemblances, while if we say they are not, we may find another thing common, or another set of family resemblances; and if we say we simply do not know, how can we tell whether the answer we get by surveying the kinds of discourse we are sure about is the correct answer?

This problem, however, is not really as disabling as it appears. There are two types of case that can give rise to uncertainty, each instructive in its own way, but neither invalidating the procedure I suggested. First, we may be unsure whether to classify a work as literary because, although we know what properties would lead us to do so, we do not know whether it has those properties. Second, we may know what properties it has, but be unsure whether those properties are literary ones. In the first case, we are unsure whether the work has a certain similarity with the works we are sure are literary discourses, but confident what sort of similarity we are looking for. In the second, we are simply unsure what sort of likeness to look for. Thus we might, in the first case, feel sure that if Plato's *Symposium* was an imaginative work, it would be a literary one, but be uncertain whether it was in the appropriate sense imaginative. In the second case, we might be sure it was imaginative, but doubt whether that was the quality we relied on in our unhesitating classification of *King Lear*, *Ulysses*, etc. as literary works.

Having distinguished the two kinds of case, we can see that the first of them is not really troublesome at all. For the problem is merely one of deciding whether a particular instance falls under a general rule or not, and that is not a problem about the rule itself. So if our aim is, as it is, to make explicit the rule implicit in our use of the expression 'literary discourse', the first type of case is irrelevant; whether or not a particular instance falls under a rule can have no bearing on the explication of the rule.

It is the second type of case that is the more interesting one, although that, too, provides no insuperable difficulty for our procedure. For what the second type of case indicates is simply that we may be able to apply a word confidently to a fairly wide range of instances without being able to say confidently what it is about those instances that leads us to apply the word to them; and that there may, therefore, be other instances to which we are uncertain whether to apply the word or not. What we should do, surely, is examine the instances in which we are sure and discover what it is about them – whether a common property (or properties) or set of family resemblances – that leads us to apply the word confidently in their case. We can then apply the knowledge that we thereby gain to the instances about which we were uncertain. The attempt at definition might then lead, through the explication of the rules implicit in our confident application of words, to a decision about the instances we were intuitively unsure of. Definitional effort might thus produce, not simply elucidation, but also refinement of our usage.

And now we can see the error underlying the suspicion that there was something wrong with the procedure I suggested we should adopt. The error lay in supposing that we must be able to say with certainty on every occasion whether something is or is not a literary discourse before we could even start looking for the properties by virtue of which we called things literary discourses. This is an error because, in the case of uncertainty about which properties warrant the application of the word, what is necessary is only that there should be some cases to which we are certain the word does apply. We do not have to decide doubtful instances before we start to define our usage; on the contrary, we may be able to let our explication of the certain instances decide the doubtful ones. Now, at last, we can get on with the search for a definition of 'literary discourse'.

Can we formulate a definition which specifies necessary and sufficient conditions for the application of the term? Several attempts have been made this century, some barely rising above the level of unelaborated suggestions, others supported by reasoned argument. But I do not think any of them succeeds and, while no single failure is decisive, the cumulative weight of many depresses confidence in ultimate success. For where the most promising candidates fail, hopes for the rest can hardly be high. Let us consider some of the best known of these attempts.

A formalist definition

There is a tradition associated with what are now known as the Russian, subsequently Czech, Formalists, which seeks to define literary discourses, or literariness, in terms of a contrast between a norm and a deviation. The contrast has been variously conceived: sometimes the norm is 'practical' language, and the deviation is 'poetic' language; sometimes the norm is poetic language, and the deviation is a new form of poetic language, intended to replace the old one that has become stale. 'Poetic language' is usually taken to mean, not simply the language used in poetry but those uses of language, or 'devices', in poetry or prose, by means of which things which the audience normally perceives, or thinks of, in habitual ways become 'defamiliarised', so that it sees, or thinks of, them in a fresh light, or with 'intensified perception'.[4]

Although these seminal views have produced a dense growth of theoretical plants, it is clear they do not formulate necessary or sufficient conditions for the application of the expression 'literary discourse'. In the first place, we can disregard the view which contrasts standard with deviant *poetic* language, for that specifies a distinction between types of *literary* discourses, not between literary and *nonliterary* ones. But the distinction between practical and poetic language serves no better as the kind of definition we are looking for. To start with, if we consider the function of the 'devices' that are supposed to define poetic language, there is no clear explanation of what 'defamiliarisation' or 'intensified perception' means (and we would, I think, be hard put to provide one), so that the definition slithers towards vacuous obscurity. Certainly, as it stands, the condition it proposes is neither necessary nor sufficient. Not necessary, for W. H. Davies's poem *Leisure*[5] certainly is literature, whether or not we think highly of it, but it does not appear to 'defamiliarise' or 'intensify perception' any more than many a nonliterary discourse might. Not sufficient, for the technical arguments, littered with mathematical formulae, in Russell and Whitehead's *Principia Mathematica* surely 'defamiliarised' or 'intensified' the audience's perception of the subject, yet it certainly is not literature. In the second place, it is clear that this is a definition of (what the Formalists regard as) good literature, not just literature; for indifferent poems, novels and plays would presumably fail to defamiliarise or bring about intensified perception, yet they would still be classified as (indifferent) literature, and it is 'literature' in the neutral sense of the term, let us remind ourselves, that we are trying to explicate. This defect could not be remedied by qualifying the definition to read: 'Literary discourses (or discourses with the property of literariness) are those in which devices do, or are *intended* to, defamiliarise or intensify perception.' For that would imply, what is plainly false, that we cannot tell whether a bad poem is a literary discourse until we know what some of the author's intentions were. Finally, if we take poetic language, not in terms of its alleged function to defamiliarise or intensify perception, but strictly in terms of linguistic deviance from the norm of practical language, and even if we ignore the difficulty of defining 'norm' here, the definition still will not provide a necessary and sufficient condition of literariness. There are stories told in a plain, ordinary ('practical') style, so it is not a necessary condition; and a scientific treatise written by a non-native speaker of English might be deviant in many ways without being literature, so it is not a sufficient condition, either. Taken merely as linguistic deviance, then, this form of the definition is also patently wrong.

The trouble here is one that is drearily familiar to students of aesthetics. A property that can with some plausibility be attributed to certain literary works, and which may become the slogan of a new literary movement, has been rudely thrust into the role of the defining characteristic of all literary works. And the consequence is confusion and distortion.

A structuralist approach

The views of literary structuralists, who are partly the progeny of Russian formalism, need scarcely detain us here. For structuralism in literature is more a loosely related set of ideas about how to analyse literary works than an attempt to define literary discourses.[6] The view that literary works are linguistic or semantic structures obviously does nothing to distinguish literary from such nonliterary linguistic structures as a chemistry text book or even a phone directory. It has, indeed, been claimed that 'speech' does not, while 'literature' does, exhibit structures higher than those of the sentence (where 'speech' means nonliterary language).[7] But that is surely false. Any linguistic composition, literary or not, may exhibit such structures. It is worth pausing, however, to notice that at least one claim of literary structuralism – the claim that literary works all have the same sort of structure that sentences of a language have, which might conceivably be thought to provide at least part of a definition – is as fallacious as it is fanciful. A literary, and for that matter any other, discourse is a concatenation of sentences, but it does not follow from this that, as has actually been suggested by Roland Barthes, the work itself is a sort of megasentence, to be analysed in megagrammatical categories that are homological with (at least) some of the grammatical categories in which the sentences that compose it are to be analysed.[8] We might as well argue that, since a queue is a concatenation of persons, it follows that it is itself a megaperson, exhibiting the same structures that the persons who compose it exhibit. It is conceivable, of course, though barely so, that the linguistic categories of sentence analysis can be usefully translated to the analysis of literary discourses. But there is no *a priori* reason to think they are more appropriate there than is any other set of categories. A dogmatic attachment to the belief that they are peculiarly appropriate, bolstered by arguments as flimsy as the one I have just quoted, can lead only to artificiality and, once again, distortion. Besides, since those categories could equally well be applied to nonliterary works, their applicability to literary ones could not serve to distinguish literary works from the rest.

In so far as structuralism does say anything at all about the definition of literature, it is probably by way of such claims as that literature 'is something animated by special sets of conventions' or that it 'is an institution composed of a variety of interpretive operations',[9] which seem to point towards a definition like that of the institutional theories which I shall discuss later in this chapter. Since those theories are clearer and more developed than the structuralists' suggestions, it is best to regard the suggestions as primitive versions of institutional theories, which we therefore need not discuss here.

A *Rezeptionaesthetik* definition

There is one development, or part-development, of Structuralism, *Rezeptionaesthetik* ('the aesthetics of reception'), which has led some theorists to attempt a genuine definition of literature. The definition is couched in semantic terms. A literary work (or 'text') is said to be one that has *Multivalenz*, or 'a multiplicity of varying, contrasting and, to a certain degree, mutually exclusive strands of meaning, which stand on an equal footing as far as validity is concerned.' 'Meaning' is understood in an extended sense here, to cover not only the meanings of words, phrases and sentences, but also all that would count as an interpretation of the work. Other writers, in the hermeneutic tradition, have similarly referred to 'openness' as a 'criterion' of literary discourses.[10]

But, again, these remarks will not do as definitions in terms of necessary and sufficient conditions; counter-examples come quickly to mind. A political speech may be (intentionally) ambiguous and capable of different, but equally valid interpretations; it may have – and may be intended to have – the property of openness, but it will not therefore be a literary work. A ballad may be simple and direct, having less multiplicity of meaning than the political speech, but still be a literary work. Clearly, this characterisation will not separate literary from nonliterary works any better than the Formalist formula did.

A 'speech act' definition of 'imaginative literature'

A more sustained attempt to work out a definition has been made by Monroe Beardsley, an attempt that incorporates a definition of imaginative or fictional works that has grown out of the theory of speech acts developed in recent analytic philosophy.[11] Beardsley distinguishes between a central concept of literature (imaginative literature): poems, novels, stories and plays; and an extended concept: some essays, sermons, speeches, etc., and he offers accordingly a disjunctive definition, the two disjuncts of which, however, are claimed to be related as two forms of the same thing. Before considering his account, we need to look briefly at the theory of speech acts on which it is partly based.[12]

Whenever people utter sentences, they are normally performing variously hierarchically related actions. They are making sounds or marks; they are uttering words in a certain grammatical construction; they are uttering those words with a certain sense and reference. Thus the sentence 'Boris is a crafty politician' is, first, a sequence of written marks (or, if spoken, of sounds); second, it is a sentence formulated according to the rules of English grammar; third, the words of the sentence have a certain sense ('crafty' has the sense of 'cunning') and reference ('Boris' refers to Yeltsin, not Godunov). The actions performed in uttering the sentence are hierarchically arranged in the sense that you cannot perform the last without performing the others, and you cannot perform the second without performing the first. The act constituted by the performance of all three acts is called a 'locutionary' act. But whenever you perform a locutionary act, you are normally also performing another kind of act as well: one of stating, asking, ordering, swearing, pleading, promising, declaring, etc. (In the example just given, for instance, the utterer is stating, not swearing. Put a question mark at the end, or give it an interrogative intonation, and it becomes a question.) This other kind of act, which is performed in the act of performing a locutionary act, is dubbed an 'illocutionary' act. Standard linguistic intercourse, therefore, consists of the performance of illocutionary acts, constituted in the way I have described. I state something to you, or ask you something, or request, promise, beg, judge, etc. You question me, deny what I say, refuse, concede, concur, etc. In each case, we are performing illocutionary acts, acts which depend on the rules of our language and also upon certain nonlinguistic conventions and conditions. Unless I am a clergyman, for instance, or entitled in some other way to perform Christian baptism, I cannot christen your baby 'Dawn' just by saying the words 'I name this child Dawn (although doing so would be performing a perfectly good locutionary act); for the relevant nonlinguistic convention has not been observed. Nor do I succeed in promising you that I will marry you, even though I perform a perfectly good locutionary act of saying 'I promise to marry you', if you do not hear me; for the relevant condition (of being heard, or 'securing uptake') is not satisfied.

Beardsley's attempt to define imaginative literature exploits this theory of illocutionary acts. He builds on, and endorses, an earlier account of the same sort put forward by R. Ohmann.[13] How do Ohmann and Beardsley use speech-act theory as the basis of such a definition? By pointing out in the first place that utterances of fictional sentences are not standard illocutionary acts. In a story beginning 'Once upon a time there was a little girl called Red Riding Hood', the author, or the teller, is not genuinely asserting that at some time a person by the name of Red Riding Hood actually existed. He cannot be accused of lying if no such person ever existed, nor can he be praised for accuracy or veracity if it happens that a person of that name really did exist; for he is not performing the illocutionary act of stating or asserting at all. What is he doing? According to Ohmann, 'A literary work purportedly imitates (or reports) a series of speech acts which in fact have no other existence.' Such works are said to have 'mimetic illocutionary force'. As it stands, this is not only not very clear, but also apparently false. The teller of the tale 'Little Red Riding Hood' is not purportedly imitating or reporting a speech act, if that means, as it apparently does, *pretending* to imitate or report one. He might, perhaps, be said to be pretending to *assert* that there was once a little girl called Red Riding Hood, a pretence which is, of course, not deceptive, but one in which the audience, as Ohmann notes, itself collaborates – they join in the pretence. But he surely is not pretending to *imitate* or 'report' any speech act, not even one that has 'no other existence.' Nor is it the literary work which pretends, as Ohmann suggests; if there is any pretence, it must be done by a conscious agent, for only conscious agents can pretend. Also there is no such thing as the illocutionary force, or act, of pretending. Merely to pretend to perform the illocutionary act of asserting is no more to perform another type of illocutionary act than merely to pretend to commit the crime of murder is to commit another type of crime. Beardsley, in his own account, notices this last point, and it is also noticed by John Searle, whose own somewhat later

26

account of fictional (not literary or imaginative) discourse – which we will consider in Chapter 3 – also gives an analysis in terms of nondeceptive pretence.

Beardsley thinks that a revised pretence analysis (as I shall call it) will yield a satisfactory definition of the 'central' concept of literature – imaginative literature. But what is imaginative literature? Beardsley mentions novels, poetry, plays, stories. He claims that what makes them imaginative literature is that they are all fiction. But we must interpret 'fiction' pretty liberally here, to include not only what we would normally call fiction (nondocumentary stories and plays) but also imaginary addresses to skylarks, Nature and mythical creatures, imaginary pleadings with fond lovers and coy mistresses, etc. These are all thought to be works of imaginative literature because they are all in some sense fictional; the persons, objects or situations are imaginary, not real. The definition offered of fictional discourse is that it is discourse in which the author nondeceptively pretends to perform illocutionary acts. The novelist pretends to report something; the poet pretends to address a skylark, the West wind, or an absent lover.

Whatever we may think of the pretence analysis, Beardsley's definition can hardly be correct as it stands. For fictional works do not consist exclusively of fictional sentences. A novel is a fictional work, for instance, but not every sentence in the novel need be a fictional sentence. The authors of novels occasionally speak in authorial asides, commenting on the story, or offering their observations on matters in general. The opening sentence of *Anna Karenina*: 'All happy families resemble one another, but each unhappy family is unhappy in its own way', may be an example of this. But such sentences are still part of the novel, part of the work. The same is true for poetry. Shakespeare may not have been addressing a real lover (though how do we know?) when he wrote 'Shall I compare thee to a summer's day?' But he may have been stating, not as Beardsley would say, pretending to state, when he added 'Rough winds do shake the darling buds of May.' If he was then making a genuine assertion, it was not an interruption, but an integral part, of the poem.

What Beardsley calls fictional works do not have to consist entirely of fictional sentences, and Beardsley's definition, even if we accepted that fiction involved pretence, would have to be amended. No doubt that could be done, but any revised version of it would still yield some pretty queer results. Elizabeth Barrett Browning's sonnet, 'How do I love thee? Let me count the ways'[14] was apparently addressed to her husband, Robert. It does not appear to be a pretended illocutionary act of addressing him: on the contrary, it seems to be a genuine one, only one that was performed in verse (there are many such works: Milton's sonnet to Vane or Cyriac Skinner, for example,[15]) and that would mean, on Beardsley's theory, that, not being fictional, the poem did not fall under the central concept of literature – and yet, if it had been addressed to an imaginary being, it would, without any

27

change of meaning, have fallen under the central concept after all. We started off assuming that poems all fall under the central concept of literature; now we are compelled to think that many do not. This is certainly odd; our intuition, surely is that Elizabeth's poem would be no less a work of imaginative literature for being addressed to Robert than it would have been if it had been addressed to some fictional person. The distinction Beardsley's theory forces us to draw is artificial.

Beardsley tries to avoid this unwelcome consequence by claiming that, despite appearances, such works are not, after all, genuine but pretended, illocutionary acts. In his sense of the term, they are fictional, he says. Why? Because there was no 'uptake' at the time of composition (Robert was not listening to or reading the words Elizabeth composed), and because 'the process of formalising a sentiment in verse and rhyme, giving it artistic shape, implies a degree of detachment from the illocutionary role'.[16]

These claims are unpersuasive. Whether there was uptake at the time of composition is irrelevant to whether it was a pretended illocutionary act or not. So long as the poem was intended for Robert, the act of writing it was not a pretended illocutionary one. True, if Robert never received or read it, uptake was not secured, and the act was flawed. But being flawed is not the same as being pretended, and whatever may be meant by 'detachment from the illocutionary role', there is no reason to suppose that because one takes care to formalise one's sentiment in verse and rhyme, one is therefore only pretending to perform the illocutionary act of asserting that one has that sentiment. Ardent patriots who sing their national anthems with their hands on their breasts are genuinely expressing their sentiments even though those sentiments are formalised in verse and rhyme.

We are left, then, with this uncomfortable consequence of defining the central concept of literature in terms of fiction in Beardsley's sense: whether a work falls under the central concept depends not on whether or not it is a poem, but on whether or not it is a *fictional* poem. Suppose we stoically endure this discomfort; what then? It seems we should next ask ourselves whether or not Beardsley's analysis of fiction in terms of pretended illocutionary acts is correct. I shall postpone that issue to the next chapter, in which I shall try to provide a more detailed account of fiction than would be appropriate here. We can provisionally agree now with Beardsley that some works are literature (whether good or bad) because they are works of fiction. What about works that are not fiction? We have to turn now to the other half of his definition, the half which covers the 'extended' concept of literature.

The 'extended concept' of literature

Beardsley offers a 'semantic' definition of literature in the extended sense, a definition which is similar in its general aim to that offered by *Rezeptionaesthetik* theorists for the whole of literature. It is that ('extended') literary works are 'those discourses a substantial part of whose meaning is implicit (or secondary) meaning', or those discourses which are 'distinctly above the norm in ratio of implicit to explicit meaning'. What is the connection between these two types of literature? Beardsley's answer is that both are 'forms of verbal play'.[17] (They could not, however, be two species of one genus, since no member of one species can be a member of another species of that genus, whereas, presumably, the same work might exhibit both a high degree of implicit meaning and also be a work of fiction.)

We might wonder what exactly 'verbal play' means here, and whether this disjunctive definition does not imply the extraordinary view that there is no closer relationship between works of 'central' and 'extended' literature than there is between quadrupeds and carnivores, which are also two different forms of the same thing – animals – and forms that can coincide in the same individual (a wolf, for instance). As if 'literature' were like some such hybrid word as *carniquad*, which we might invent to designate animals which were either carnivores or quadrupeds (or both). But we can forgo these speculations. For the semantic definition is as flawed as the *Rezeptionaesthetik* one it resembles, and so Beardsley's definition must fail as a whole.

What is implicit, or secondary meaning? What is the norm? Implicit meaning is the suggestions and connotations carried by particular words, forms of syntax, phrases and sentences, or the tone and context of a whole discourse. Thus Elizabeth Browning's use of 'thee' in 'How do I love thee?' suggests, according to Beardsley, that she is at the very least familiar with the person addressed. The word 'sea' connotes, variously, danger, moodiness, tranquillity, motion, a barrier, a thoroughfare, and so on, while in particular contexts it will connote only some of these things, as perhaps in Masefield's 'I must go down to the sea again.' The syntax of 'Napoleon, who recognised the danger to his right flank, himself led his Guards against the enemy position' suggests that Napoleon led his Guards against the enemy *after* and *because* he recognised the danger, although that is not actually stated. The line 'And summer's lease hath all too short a date' suggests that summer is granted to us like something we borrow or rent. Finally, many of Graham Greene's novels, or Kierkegaard's *Fear and Trembling* may suggest by their tone and content that life is often a fairly wretched business.

All discourses have implicit or secondary meaning, but some have more than others. The higher the ratio of implicit to explicit meaning in a discourse, according to the theory, the more literary the discourse. The norm is thus not a fixed amount, but a blurry-edged band in a spectrum. Some discourses are high in implicit meaning, and they are literary (in the extended sense). Others are low, and they are not. There are still others about which we may be unsure. The norm is, moreover, relative to the type of discourse. The amount of secondary or implicit meaning that is the norm in a logic text book is likely to be much less than that which is the norm in a work of biography or history.[18]

The essence of the theory is that the possession of a distinctly higher than average amount of secondary or implicit meaning for the type of discourse in question is a necessary and sufficient condition of the work's being a literary one in the extended sense of the term. But, unfortunately, it is not. So far from providing a necessary or sufficient condition, the account leads to absurdity. For how, on this account, are we to classify a poem like Elizabeth Browning's 'How do I love thee?'? What type of discourse does it belong to – poetry, sonnets, love poetry, Victorian poetry, love letters, Elizabeth Browning's poetry? The choice even so far is bewildering, and it is by no means exhaustive. We can choose what we like, and so fix a norm; then, by some classifications, the sonnet will turn out to be a literary work, while by others it will not. This is surely absurd.

Suppose we amend the account, then. Suppose we drop the idea that the norm is relative to a type of discourse, and say simply that a discourse is literary if most of its meaning is secondary or implicit meaning. Then suppose we allow, rather generously, that we can compare 'amounts' of meaning in this way. Still we end in absurdity. For what is being proposed is a scale of literariness determined by the ratio of implicit to explicit meaning. It follows from this that the more implicit meaning a work has, the more literary it becomes. Elizabeth Browning's sonnet is, perhaps, just, a work of extended literature in that case (as we have seen, it will not qualify by Beardsley's criteria as a work of central literature), but less so than Sir Thomas Browne's *Urn Burial*, which carries a much heavier freight of implicit meaning. while Philip Larkin's poem *Places, Loved Ones*, or R. D. Laing's *Eight*,[19] neither of which appears to be addressed to or about imaginary people or situations, and hence neither of which will apparently fall under the central concept of literature, will not qualify as extended literature, either – here, if anywhere, there is more explicit than implicit meaning in the sense Beardsley gives to those terms. Yet *Places, Loved Ones*, and *Eight* are certainly literary works, whether good or bad, and not the less so for having more explicit than implicit meaning.

These examples show that the semantic definition does not provide a necessary condition of a nonfictional work's being literary. It is equally clear, though, that it does not provide a sufficient condition, either. We noticed earlier, when we were considering the *Rezeptionaesthetik* account of literature, that an ill-written thesis or a political speech might contain a multiplicity of meanings, and yet not be a literary discourse. The same objection holds for Beardsley's theory. Such different discourses as a casual letter to a friend, or a slangy report of a football match may carry more implicit than explicit meaning. Possibly most nontechnical discourse does so; certainly many ordinary conversations contain more suggestions, connotations, innuendoes and hints than remarks to be taken only in their literal meaning, and they may well suggest a view of life or some aspect of life. But none of these things is sufficient to make them literary discourses. We do not produce literature every time we casually open our mouths.

An institutional definition

This attempt fails, too, then. Its failure may prompt us to look in a different direction. We have been searching for features that authors confer on their discourses: multiplicity of meaning, fictional subjects or modes, special devices. But perhaps that is the wrong way to go about it? The last type of definition I shall consider is one that claims we have indeed been looking in the wrong place. Accordingly, it considers *the way we treat* what an author produces, rather than the *features of his products*. George Dickie has advanced a definition of the generic term 'work of art' (in the neutral sense) as follows:[20] 'A work of art is an artifact, upon (some aspects of) which a person or persons acting on behalf of a certain social institution (the art world) has conferred the status of candidate for appreciation'. Adapting this formula to the specific case of literature, we get: a literary work is a discourse, upon (some aspects of) which a person or persons acting on behalf of a certain social institution (the literature world) has conferred the status of candidate for appreciation.

What exactly does this mean? A certain impreciseness of expression makes it difficult to say with confidence, particularly as the definition seems to have been conceived originally with works of visual art in mind. But I believe what follows is as close as we can get. The literature world is a social institution consisting of various practices: the composing, publishing, reading or hearing and criticising of various discourses such as poems, plays, novels, essays, etc. If a discourse is published (in good faith) as a novel or a poem, it thereby has the status of candidate for appreciation conferred on it. But the same status could be conferred on a discourse by anyone acting as an agent of the literature world, whether the discourse was published or not. In composing *Urn Burial*, Sir Thomas Browne might not have conferred the status of candidate for appreciation upon it – he might not, that is, have been acting as an agent of the literature world, he might not have wished to confer that status on his discourse. But someone who did act as an agent of the literature world (a subsequent critic, for instance), might treat the work in such a way that the status was thereby conferred upon it. On the other hand, an always unpublished author who locks his work away in his desk can himself confer the status on his own discourse in the very act of composing it as a novel or poem. For if someone conceives of his discourse as a novel or poem, he thereby acts on behalf of the literary world; and a work need not in fact be appreciated for the status of *candidate* for appreciation to be conferred upon it.

This is a radical suggestion; but its boldness cannot compensate for the obscurity of its details. What exactly is the literature world? Can the word 'literature' (in 'literature world') be eliminated from the definition so as to avoid circularity? How does one contrive to act on behalf, or as an agent, of it? Which actions do, and which do not, count as conferring the status of candidate for appreciation on discourses? Does a discourse have to have some feature in virtue of which one confers the status of candidate for appreciation on it, as people normally have to have some quality in virtue of which one confers a title on them? Or is it, rather, like conferring a name on a child or a pet? Neither daughters nor dogs need have some special feature to distinguish them from other daughters and dogs in order to get the names they do – their parents or owners may simply pick the name out of a hat. Dickie himself says the act of conferring the status is 'rather like' christening – which suggests there does not have to be a special feature. Moreover, he says that if one sees oneself as an agent of the literature world, then one is one. Can I confer the status of candidate for appreciation on a plumber's manual just because I see myself as an agent of the literature world, and happen to feel like it, and thereby make the manual a literary work?

All these issues would have to be clarified before we could assess the worth of this definition, were it not for the fact that there is, in any case, a decisive objection against it. The objection concerns the meaning of the word 'appreciation'. What kind of appreciation is it that is relevant here? The kind 'characteristic of our experiences of … poetry, novels and the like', Dickie suggests. To the objection that our appreciation of these things may have nothing in common, he replies that 'if we mean by 'appreciation' something like 'in experiencing the qualities of a thing one finds them worthy or valuable', then there is no problem about the similarity of the various appreciations'.[21] Neglecting grammatical anomalies about this gloss, we can, perhaps, say that the idea is that in conferring the status of candidate for appreciation on a discourse, we are declaring that it is something to be considered from the point of view of whether, in experiencing its qualities, one finds them worthy or valuable. But this is obviously too wide; there must be some restriction on the qualities that we are to take into account in considering whether in experiencing them we find them worthy or valuable. If you consider a discourse from the point of view of whether you find its qualities of being solely about sheepfarming, or written in the Scottish Borders dialect of the nineteenth century, worthy or valuable in experiencing them, you will not be considering the discourse as literature. The discourse will be a candidate for appreciation, certainly, but not for that appreciation which is characteristic of our appreciation of poetry, novels and the like.

We shall then have to return from the gloss to the original definition. The status to be conferred must be that of candidate for appreciation 'of the kind characteristic of our experiences of poetry, novels and the like'. This eliminates the wrong kind of appreciation, but it resurrects the problem that the gloss was meant to solve. What is characteristic of those experiences? Clearly, it will not do to say merely that they are all cases of literary appreciation, for we need to know what it is that makes them all instances of literary appreciation. If we are not told, the purported definition remains incomplete. It is as if one were to define 'officer cadet' as 'a person upon whom someone acting on behalf of the officer world has conferred the status of candidate for the rank of officer', but was unable to give a definition of 'officer'. Remember that this institutional definition is intended, like the others we have considered, to provide necessary and sufficient conditions for the application of the term 'literary discourse'. Unless it can provide necessary and sufficient conditions for the application of the term 'literary appreciation' which forms part of the alleged definition, it must also fail to provide them for the application of the term 'literary discourse'. Dickie does not provide them, and as I can see no way in which this deficiency can be made good, I conclude that his definition cannot be repaired.

The social practice theory

A rather different institutional theory has been proposed by S. H. Olsen. According to this view, literature is a social practice not merely in:

> the minimal sense that it involves a group of people among whom literary works are produced and read, but also in the stricter sense that it is a practice whose existence depends on a background of concepts and conventions which create the possibility of identifying literary works and provide a framework for appreciation, and on the people actually applying these concepts and conventions in their approach to literary works ... A literary work must ... be seen as being offered to an audience by an author with the intention that it should be understood with reference to a shared background of concepts and conventions which must be employed to determine its aesthetic features. A reader must be conceived of as a person who approaches the work with a set of expectations defined in terms of these concepts and conventions. Somebody who did not share this institutional background would not be able to identify aesthetic features in it because he did not know the concepts and conventions which define these features.[22]

There must exist, Olsen seems to be claiming, a number of works which count canonically as literary works and a pattern of argument by which the presence of literary aesthetic features is established, before there can be any such thing as literature. As it stands, this claim appears circular; it seems to assert that literature cannot exist unless it already does, for literary works are simply what literature is. But, waiving that point, it may well be trivially true that, if we understand by 'literature' the *social institution* involving the practice of intentionally producing linguistic compositions for assessment as

33

literary works, we cannot have literature without a background of conventions and concepts of the kind Olsen adumbrates – that, after all, is what the social institution is. But, since that does not entail that compositions having the features, whatever they are, characteristic of literary works cannot exist independently of those conventions and concepts, it would be a mistake (if that is indeed what Olsen intends) to try to build this feature into the definition of literature. A person might conceivably produce sentences exhibiting rhythm, rhyme, metaphor, imaginary addresses, and whatever other features we may consider characteristic of poetry, in a society where previously no such features had ever appeared. We may even suppose that the sentences were identical with those constituting a poem by some poet in another society which spoke the same language, but had no contact whatsoever with the first one. There could surely be no doubt that the person had produced a poem, although the *social institution* of literature did not exist in his society. It would not, of course, be classified as a poem, and hence would not be criticised as one; but that would not affect its status as a poem, nor even its having a typically 'poetic' effect on its audience. It would be a poem because of the features it possessed, not because there were people who recognised and appreciated the features it possessed.

That is not to deny that literary works are usually produced in a social setting, with a background of shared concepts and conventions. Clearly, that is so. But the existence of at least some literary works does not logically depend on the institutional circumstances commonly surrounding their production. Hence a definition of *literary work* which postulates a logical connection between the social practices typical of the institution of literature and the existence of an individual work must be wrong.

A 'family resemblance' approach

We can hardly survey this register of attempted definitions without feeling some loss of confidence. Tzetvan Todorov, indeed, after conducting a lively tour of the ruins of various attempts to define literature in some of the ways we have just considered, wondered resignedly whether 'literature does not exist' (that is, whether there is no univocal meaning of 'literature' at all).[23] This resignation rests on an assumption: that it can exist only if we can define it in the traditional way, by specifying necessary and sufficient conditions. But that assumption, as we have already noted, may be false. We have not exhausted all our resources yet, and, if we cannot find some property common to all and only the things we call literary discourses, it no more follows that literature does not exist than it follows that, if we cannot find some property common to all and only the things we call amusing (apart, of course, from the fact that we do call them all amusing), amusement does not exist. If we have failed to find such a property, perhaps we should now look in a different direction: not for yet another alleged common property, but for different, overlapping ones. Instead of asking 'What do all literary works have in common?', let us rather ask 'What is it in each case that justifies our calling something a literary discourse (regardless of whether it is common to all other literary discourses or not)?' This is, of course, to attempt a 'family resemblance' characterisation of literature.[24]

Consider some of the examples of literature that we have cited already. Why do we classify *The Waste Land, Ulysses, Day of the Jackal*, The Sermon On The Mount, *Urn Burial, King Lear* and *George the Big Engine* all as literature (in the neutral sense)? There seems to be no single property or properties which they all and only they have in common, by virtue of which we call them literature. Yet, if asked to justify our application of the word to them, we could cite properties by virtue of which we applied the term in each case. Some of them are metrical – that is, they have a stress pattern, with or without rhyme, more regular than that of ordinary speech (*The Waste Land*, The Sermon on the Mount). Others are fictions (*George the Big Engine, Ulysses, The Waste Land*), some are fictions and metrical (*The Waste Land, King Lear*). Some are in unusually figurative language compared with discourses that we would not call literary (*Urn Burial*, The Sermon on the Mount).

These are the features we would cite, some in one case, some in another, to vindicate our calling them all literature. Some have several of the features, others only one. *King Lear* and *The Waste Land* have them all, the others have not. *Day Of The Jackal* and *George the Big Engine* are like *King Lear* in being fictions, but in them the feature of being metrical has diminished or gone. *Ulysses* retains some (prose) metre and figurative language, while *Day Of The Jackal* and *George the Big Engine* have less or none. The Sermon on the Mount is like *King Lear* and *The Waste Land* in using figurative language, but here the feature of being fictional, which *The Waste Land, George the Big Engine, King Lear* and *Day Of The Jackal* each in its own way possesses, has dropped away. Philip Larkin's *Dawn* is like *King Lear* and *The Waste Land* in being metrical, but, as with W. H. Davies's *Leisure* the feature of being fictional has gone, as has that of preponderantly figurative language, and if we look at other discourses, we find that it is by virtue of some or other, or all, of these features that we apply the word 'literary' to them. *On the Nature of Things* has the feature of figurative language, and is metrical. *Ward Number Six* is fiction, although figurative language drops mostly away. Demosthenes's *Philippics* has figurative language and prose metre, but is not fiction. A story in *Just Seventeen* is fiction but makes little use of figurative language or prose rhythms.

Consider now discourses about which we might hesitate: Gibbon's *Decline and Fall of the Roman Empire*, perhaps. If we are uncertain whether this is a literary work, what is the reason? Surely we are wondering about such things as whether Gibbon's sentences have sufficiently metrical a pattern, whether they are sufficiently constructed to exploit the sound of their words, whether there is enough figurative language, to justify us in classifying his work as literature. With Carlyle's *French Revolution*, we may have less doubt. (Of course, to say this is not to say that Carlyle's book may be better than Gibbon's; only that his work may exhibit more qualities from the literary domain, whether we find them good or bad instances of those qualities.)

I have mentioned some of the features which we would cite to justify our calling a discourse (in the neutral sense) a literary one. Let us look at them more closely. There are some features that concern auditory and to some limited extent visual features of language, such as rhyme, metre (whether strict or 'free') onomatopoeia, alliteration, and eye rhymes. There are related features, such as anaphora and epistrophe. There are broadly 'figurative' features – a heterogeneous category – not dependent on sound or look, such as metaphor (including synecdoche and metonymy), simile, meiosis, irony and hyperbole, and there is fiction.

Constellations of these features, or sometimes just one of them alone, can yield a reason for calling a discourse a literary work. We are justified in doing so if it is fictional: that is, if it is a continuous narrative discourse consisting for the most part of fictional sentences. If it has largely figurative language – a preponderance of similes and metaphors, for example – again we are justified in calling it a literary work. Finally, if it is in verse, or if its sentences, though not in verse, have a distinct ('prose') metre, and it has a preponderance of other auditory and perhaps visual qualities, once again we have reason to describe it as a literary work. Discourses which we call literary possess some of these features, and it is because they possess one, or some mix, of them that we call them literary. Whether a work is literary can, of course, be a matter of uncertainty, for each of these categories admits of degree. A discourse may have literary qualities without being a literary discourse: it may have some of them, but not enough to preclude hesitation or disagreement over its classification. Or sometimes it may not be clear whether it really has them. (You cannot always tell immediately, for instance, whether a discourse is fictional or not. That a work is billed as a novel does not guarantee that it is fiction, while that it is billed as autobiography does not guarantee that it is not. In each case we may lack the means to decide which it is.)

Since literary discourses usually have some mix of the kind of features mentioned above, they will usually exhibit various overlapping and crisscrossing resemblances to each other in the way characteristic of family resemblance terms, although sometimes there will be only one feature in common with some other literary works (being fictional, for example). But it is because of these resemblances, not because of one single omnipresent feature or set of features, that we apply the term 'literary' to each of them. Some works possess a large number of the features we have discussed – *King Lear*, for instance. They are fictional, figurative, and have rhyme and metre.

36

Others have fewer – *Urn Burial* is not fictional, *George the Big Engine* has neither figurative nor rhythmical language. Not that this is a reason for estimating *King Lear* more highly than *George the Big Engine*. A discourse that is threefold literary is not therefore three times as good a work of literature as one that is not. *King Lear* may, indeed, succeed or fail in more ways than *George the Big Engine*, just as an athlete who enters for three events may succeed or fail in more ways than an athlete who enters only for one. But that of itself does not mean that *King Lear* is a better work than *George the Big Engine*, any more than an athlete's entering for three events means that he is a better athlete than an athlete who enters only for one. The athlete who wins the hundred metres may be a better athlete than the one who comes third in the hundred metres, fourth in the long jump and last in the discus.

There are several distinct sources of literariness, although most literary works contain features from more than one source, and that is why attempts to define literariness in terms of necessary and sufficient conditions for the application of the term all fail. But 'literature' is not an ambiguous word like 'pen'; for the different things we call literature, unlike the different things we call pens, are all related to each other in the ways in which members of a family resemble each other – that is, variously.

There is one more point to note about the family resemblance analysis: its application to marginal cases. I have spoken all along of certain features *justifying* the application of the term 'literary'. I did not say that their presence always *mandated* the term's application. This is important. We would be simply mistaken to withhold the term from *King Lear*, but we might not be mistaken to withhold it from a joke, which is also fictional, or from a television commercial which employed actors playing parts in a brief scene intended to advertise some product. A resemblance to other things called literature is there, certainly; but we are not *required* to extend the term at the margins of its applicability. We may do so; but, in view of other features, or the lack of them, or simply because we have not felt called upon to do so, we may not. Jokes, though fictional, and acted television commercials, though dramatic, we do not normally count as literature, although we may on occasion count one or two lines of verse as literature. There is, admittedly, a certain haphazardness about this; but only regimental minds will find this irksome. Some cities have streets laid out on a preconceived plan, others have streets that grow higgledy-piggledy over the years as a need is felt to add one or connect another – yet we can live and find our way in both. Language is like that, too. That is how we deal with marginal cases.

Conclusion

We have now got an answer to the question posed at the beginning of this chapter. But we have not got a satisfactory analysis of fiction yet. With the exception of metaphor, which we shall consider later, and irony which we shall consider together with fiction, the literariness-conferring features of discourses are fairly straightforward, but fiction, for a start, requires a more detailed treatment. I shall undertake that in the next chapter.

3

FICTION

Prologue

Some literature is fiction, but not all fiction is literature. A wordless strip
cartoon and a mime play, if they show us imaginary characters acting in
imaginary scenes and situations, are works of fiction; but they are not
linguistic productions, and are not literature. How much does fiction cover,
then? Kendall Walton has suggested that representational paintings are as
much works of fiction as are novels, stories, plays, films and the like. Walton
says Seurat's painting *Sunday on the Island of La Grande Jatte*, for instance,
is a work of fiction.[1] It is not at all clear that this is so according to the
ordinary meaning of (the relevant sense of) 'fiction', which, the dictionary
defines broadly as 'a thing feigned or imagined'; or, more narrowly, as 'an
invented statement or narrative'. If *La Grande Jatte* is a representation of
an actual scene, it is neither a thing feigned or imagined (though imagining
may be involved in our apprehension of it), nor an invented statement or
narrative. Representational paintings (and other visual works) can only
properly be called works of fiction, if at all, when they represent imaginary
scenes. Works of fiction may, indeed, be representations, but not all representations are works of fiction. A photograph of Buckingham Palace is a
representation of it, but it is not a work of fiction. Walton, however, revises
both these terms, and advocates using 'fiction' and 'representation' inter-
changeably. I believe this is confusing and perhaps confused (I identify a
possible source of confusion in the penultimate paragraph of this chapter),
and I shall use 'fiction' in its ordinary sense here, reserving a more detailed
discussion of Walton's views for the analysis of imagination which I will
undertake later (in Chapter 5). To the extent that *La Grande Jatte* represents
an actual scene. it is not a work of fiction. To the extent that a cartoon strip,
a mime play and *Anna Karenina* represent imaginary persons and actions,
they are works of fiction. Moreover, I am going to suggest in the following
discussion that the central idea involved in the term 'work of fiction' is that
of an invented *narrative*; and that it is this idea that we need principally to
understand.

The question I want to answer in this chapter is this: What makes a discourse a work of fiction? We sometimes call lies and prevarications fictions; and, while works of fiction do not consist of lies, there is a connection between these two uses of the term. For neither lies nor works of fiction (nor sole fictional sentences) are intended to be true, (though fictional works may, nevertheless, be intended to *suggest* or *imply* highly important truths). This provides us with a startline for the analysis of fiction.

The pretended illocutionary act theory

First let us recall that works of fiction need not consist exclusively of fictional sentences – that is, as the dictionary has it, of 'invented statements'. To be a work of fiction, a discourse must contain some, and perhaps a majority, of fictional sentences; but certainly not every one of them must be so. Authors may make nonfictional asides to the reader and air their opinions on anything under the sun while conducting their narrative but, provided they do not do it too much, that does not mean that what they write is not a work of fiction. Nor does it mean that their asides are not part of the work. An author given to making such remarks does not write two works inside one cover, a work of fiction and a work of personal observation; he writes one work of fiction with his personal observations in it. No doubt a work in which the number of nonfictional sentences vastly outweighed the number of fictional ones would not qualify as a work of fiction. But there is no magic number, no exact proportion, where we cross the border. There might be cases in which we would be unsure whether to classify a discourse as fiction, even though we were perfectly sure that more than half of its sentences were fictional, and the reason would be that we have no precise idea (and do not feel the need of one) as to what proportion of a work's sentences must be fictional if the work itself is to be a work of fiction.

What is it about a sentence that makes it a fictional sentence? John Searle's answer, which I briefly alluded to in the previous chapter, runs like this.[2] There are certain conditions governing the performance of illocutionary acts that are waived when we utter fictional sentences. When, performing the illocutionary act of stating, we utter the sentence 'Jack and Jill went up the hill', we must satisfy certain conditions. The words 'Jack', 'Jill' and 'the hill', for instance, must designate, or be intended to designate, actual persons or objects; the whole predicate 'went up the hill' must be asserted of the subjects Jack and Jill; and we must utter the sentence in the belief that it is true. But if we utter the sentence as fiction, none of those conditions needs be fulfilled. No actual persons are designated, or intended to be; the predicate 'went up the hill' is not asserted of any actual persons; and we do not believe the sentence is true. That, of course, might be the case if we were telling a lie, intending to deceive our audience into thinking that there were such people, such an object and such an event, while we knew, or at least believed, there were not. What distinguishes the fictional sentence from the lie is that we do not intend to deceive our audience – on the contrary, we intend them to understand that we are not speaking, or trying to speak, the literal truth. We intend our audience to understand, according to Searle, that we are *pretending*, not trying, to report an historical event. Of course, for the utterance to be successful as fiction, our audience must understand and collude with our intention; they must pretend, too, that the utterance is a genuine statement. To this extent, Olsen's claim, discussed in Chapter 2, that the existence of literature depends on the existence of certain conventions, may be correct, even if it goes too far. Fictional sentences could not succeed in their aim unless both utterer and audience understood that there is some sort of nondeceptive pretence, or, 'make-believe', going on.

If we describe as 'standard' utterances those in which the conditions governing illocutionary acts are in force, we can say that those in which they are waived are 'nonstandard'. This does not imply any derogation of them, of course. Fictional sentences are nonstandard utterances, if Searle is right, but fictional discourses may be among the most important there are. To say they are nonstandard is to describe, not to judge, them. It is also to indicate that they are, in an entirely innocuous way, parasitic on standard sentences. If we did not understand what it is to state that Jack and Jill went up the hill, we could not understand what it is to pretend to state, or to tell a story that began 'Jack and Jill went up the hill...'

To utter a fictional sentence, according to Searle, is to perform a nonde-ceptive pretended illocutionary act, but he does not say whether he thinks the converse is true, that is, whether to perform a nondeceptive pretended illocutionary act is to utter a fictional sentence. If what he is offering us is a traditional definition, the converse would have to be true; for such a defini-tion states an equivalence – if the definition of 'man' is 'rational animal', then all men are rational animals and all rational animals are men. But it seems that either Searle is not offering us such a definition, or else it must be flawed. For the case of irony (and metaphor – but we will not discuss that here) suggests that in fact the converse is not true. Let us look briefly at irony, then.

Irony and fiction

It is common to define irony as saying one thing and meaning another, or saying something in order to convey the opposite. Thus when, in Shakespeare's *Julius Caesar*, Antony says, ironically, 'And Brutus is an honourable man',[3] it is claimed he means, or contrives to convey, that Brutus is not an honourable man at all. But there is something unsatisfactory about this account. In the first place, it does not explain what the point of such a procedure could possibly be. If Antony wants his audience to believe that Brutus is not an honourable man, why does he not just say so, instead of apparently saying that he is? In the second place, what sense of 'saying' is operative here: merely uttering the *sentence* 'Brutus is an honourable man', or also thereby making the *statement* that he is? Whichever is meant, the account is obscure. For how can we, either by uttering a sentence with the meaning that Brutus is an honourable man, or by actually asserting that sentence (and thereby making a statement to the effect that he is) manage to convey in some conventional way that he is not? If it does not tell us that, the theory does not so much solve a problem as enlarge it.

Considerations like these have led Dan Sperber and Deirdre Wilson to propose a different account.[4] According to them, a sentence uttered ironically is not being used to make a statement, ask a question, etc., but is being 'quoted'. It is being quoted for the purpose of drawing attention to the gap between the circumstances under which it would be appropriate to utter the sentence to make a statement, ask a question, etc., and the circumstances which actually prevail. Thus Antony does not *state* that Brutus is an honourable man; he *quotes the sentence* 'Brutus is an honourable man', in order to draw attention to the discrepancy between Brutus's actual conduct (as described in the speech) and the circumstances in which it would be appropriate to state that Brutus was an honourable man.

This account brings us nearer to the truth, I believe; but it does not reach it. The failure lies in the use of the idea of quotation. What is it to quote? Quoting is a form of repetition or echoing, parasitic upon uttering: we cannot quote a sentence that has not first been uttered. If I quote you, I repeat your words; and if I quote you accurately, I repeat them exactly. But, in Antony's speech, whose words are being quoted? No one's. An ironical remark may very well involve a quotation, but it need not do so. When it does, it is not the fact that a quotation is involved that creates the irony. A pupil may say 'The dog ate my essay' as an excuse for failing to hand in his assignment, and his teacher may repeat ironically 'The dog ate your essay', or (more exactly) 'The dog ate my essay.' The irony lies somewhere (still to be indicated) in the contrast between what the teacher appears to be doing – neutrally repeating the student's excuse – and what she is really doing – treating it with sceptical scorn. In any case, an ironical remark may be, and no doubt often is, original, in the sense that it is a sentence, or a thought, that is uttered for the first time on that occasion. In that case, clearly, it cannot be a quotation. Antony's 'So are they all, all honourable men'[5] might have been such a sentence.

Sperber and Wilson's account must be wrong then. But it does point us towards the truth. This is that the ironical speaker is speaking in order to achieve a certain effect which contrasts with the effect that would standardly be intended by uttering the sentence, i.e. when speaking seriously in order to make a statement. The ironist is not quoting a sentence, but uttering it nonseriously. (Perhaps I should assure some readers here that, just as 'nonstandard' was not derogatory earlier, so 'nonserious' is not now; irony is an accomplishment, not a defect.) What exactly is this effect which the ironist seeks to achieve?

Consider this example. Someone arrives an hour late for a dinner party, wearing jeans and a sweater although the invitation specified formal dress. The hostess rises from the dinner table, where the guests are already half-way through the main course, and says, in a tone that betokens her ironical intention, 'So glad you could get here on time! And perfectly dressed, as well!'

What is going on here? I suggest it is that the hostess is seeking to embarrass or make fun of the tardy and unsuitably attired guest by drawing attention to his late arrival and casual dress, in terms (to put it generally, for the moment) which exploit the incongruity between the circumstances actually prevailing and those which would normally be appropriate for uttering the words seriously, i.e. nonironically – circumstances, in other words, which would render a serious utterance of her words true.

That point we owe to Sperber and Wilson: the hostess draws attention to and exploits a contrast, for the purpose of ridicule or reproof. But it is the way in which she does it that they misunderstand. The hostess does not *quote* a sentence; she *pretends to perform a certain illocutionary act* by uttering it. She pretends, that is, to compliment the late-arriver, while all the time intending that the audience should understand that she is only pretending, and that really she is rebuking or ridiculing him by drawing attention to the gap between the actual circumstances (the guest's being late and improperly dressed) and the circumstances that would render her remark appropriate (the guest's being punctual and properly dressed). For the irony to be effective, the audience, including the person addressed, must, of course, understand her intention. In the same way, the teacher who quotes her delinquent pupil's excuse is pretending to repeat it neutrally while all along intending the audience to understand that she is not neutral at all – on the contrary, she disbelieves it – and is really mocking or reproving him. Antony, in *Julius Caesar*, pretends to be stating that Brutus is an honourable man while really drawing attention to the gap between the actual circumstances, as described in his speech, and the circumstances that would make the statement appropriate. Ironical utterances are, thus, nondeceptive pretended illocutionary acts.[6]

So the converse does not hold. Even if all fictional utterances did turn out to be nondeceptive illocutionary acts, not all nondeceptive illocutionary acts would be fictional utterances. At best Searle's account cannot be complete. Fiction and irony are different, yet his account does not explain the difference. So, even if it is right as far as it goes, it needs to go further. But is it right as far as it goes?

Revising the theory

There is little doubt that fiction involves some sort of nondeceptive pretence; so far, I think, Searle is right. The question is, though, whether he has put pretence in the right place. Gregory Currie has argued that he has not.[7] The author of fiction, Currie claims, is not 'pretending to state', for instance, that Jack and Jill went up the hill...He is, rather, merely 'uttering the sentence' 'Jack and Jill went up the hill...', and 'inviting his audience to pretend to themselves' that it is true. Such a linguistic act he calls the illocutionary act of uttering fiction. The difference between these two accounts can be stated as a difference in the speaker's intention – does he intend to nondeceptively pretend to state, or does he intend only to invite others to pretend to themselves that his words are true?

I think Currie's account is correct in one respect, and wrong in another. It is correct in its location of the essential place of pretence in the utterance of fictional sentences (although no doubt much fiction-production does in fact conform to Searle's account, too). Every act of fiction-uttering is, indeed, an act of inviting one's audience to make-believe or pretend *something* to themselves, although, as we shall see, it is not always that of inviting them to pretend that the sentences they are apprehending are true statements. It is often, it is true, also an act of pretending to state, if by that we understand pretending to oneself to state. (I am not sure whether Searle would take 'pretending to state' in this way, but it is at least a plausible adaptation of what he says.) For sometimes a storyteller may equally well either utter sentences which he invites his audience to pretend are true, while not pretending to himself that they are or, rather, utter them with the (usually) implied preface 'Let's pretend (to ourselves) that these sentences are true,' including himself as one of the self-pretenders. (I shall deal here, for simplicity's sake, with declarative sentences only. Obviously, fictional works contain many other types of sentences, such as interrogative, imperative and exclamatory sentences; but it would be tedious and otiose to qualify my remarks every time by acknowledging this fact. Such sentences can be assumed to be embedded in some such authorial phrase as 'He/she/they said', or 'asked' or 'ordered' etc.) In the first case, the author remains detached, as it were, from his fictional utterance; in the second, he does not – and in that case, pretending (to himself) that his sentences are true statements is surely pretending (to himself) that he is performing the illocutionary act of (truthfully) stating, just as pretending to myself that what I am drinking is wine is pretending to myself that I am drinking wine. This feature of fiction-uttering may be quite common, and that is, perhaps, what has misled Searle into thinking it is a defining feature of fictional sentences. Currie is right in his contention that it is not. The fiction-producer is to this extent like an actor. An actor, by means of his behaviour in the context of the theatre, invites his *audience* to pretend to themselves that he is Hamlet; he may also, although he need not, pretend to *himself* that he is.

The respect in which Currie is less palatable than Searle is in his claim that fiction-uttering is a type of illocutionary act.[8] For there simply is no illocutionary act of uttering fiction. 'Illocutionary act' is a category that collects statements, promises, questions, orders, etc., not fiction and nonfiction performances. Asking whether an utterance is fictional or not is not at all the same kind of thing as asking whether it is an order or a request, any more than asking whether your dog is a real dog or an imitation one is like asking whether it is a Spaniel or a Dalmatian. The fiction/nonfiction distinction is not a distinction between types of illocutionary acts any more than the real dog/imitation dog distinction is a distinction between breeds of dogs.

We need a perspicuous term here, to capture the distinction between what I have been calling nonstandard or nonserious utterances, which are not illocutionary acts, and those which are. Ironical and fictional utterances, we have seen, are characteristically utterances of sentences by means of which the author uses a sentence apt for performing an illocutionary act in order to perform an act of another and more sophisticated kind. Let us call such acts *para-illocutionary* acts. The ironist and the fiction-maker perform para-illocutionary acts. But there are other types of para-illocutionary acts apart from these. Lies are one type: liars typically utter a sentence in order to appear (i.e. they pretend) to be making an assertion expressing their belief, whereas in fact they are only trying to get their audience to believe to be true something which (*they* believe) is false. Metaphors are another type: someone who issues the metaphor 'Life is not a bed of roses' does not assert the glaring literal truism that life is not a bed of roses, but uses a sentence apt for making that superfluous assertion in order to perform a different and more sophisticated kind of act altogether (I shall discuss this more fully in Chapter 6).

First and third person fictional discourse

The question we have been trying to settle is how fictional discourses involve nondeceptive pretending, and the answer Currie offers is that fictional sentences are sentences the author invites the audience to pretend to themselves are true; to this we might add that when the author 'joins in the game' they may be sentences he, too, pretends to himself are true, sentences which he and the audience are jointly to make-believe are genuine illocutionary acts of (truly) stating. An advantage of this way of characterising fiction would be that it would give us one clear way of distinguishing fictional sentences from ironical ones. In an ironical 'statement', the audience are to understand the speaker is pretending, but they are not to join in the pretence – on the contrary, the irony will not work unless the audience, rather than pretending to themselves that the utterance is true, exploit their belief that the ironical remark, if uttered seriously, would be false.

Nevertheless, the theory, whether in Searle's or in Currie's form, is inadequate, for it neglects the existence of first person narratives. When we read or hear a work such as Joyce Cary's *Herself Surprised*,[9] in which the narrator, Sara, is herself a character in the fiction, we do not always make-believe or pretend to ourselves that the narrator's sentences are *true*. On the contrary, we are induced by the author's skill to conclude that sometimes she is deceiving herself or trying to deceive her audience, and that some of her sentences are not true at all. For example, when, early on, they read 'But I was not flighty then. I was a sober-sides',[10] the audience may be inclined to take the sentences as true (that is, to make-believe they are reading the words of a real person, Sara, who is speaking truthfully). But later, as the story develops, they may well come to think them false in the fiction (come, that is, to make-believe they are reading the words of a real person, Sara, who is speaking falsely).

In such first person cases, what the author invites the audience to pretend to themselves is not that the sentences they are reading or hearing are true, but only that they are sentences uttered by a real, not an imaginary, person. In other first person cases, however, such as Marguerite Yourcenar's *Memoirs of Hadrian*,[11] the audience are not to pretend to themselves that the Emperor Hadrian was a *real person*. (For they are surely supposed to know that he *was* a real person; he is a character in the fiction, but not a *fictional* character in that fiction). They are to pretend to themselves that the sentences they are reading are *genuine utterances* of that real person. Compare these two examples with cases of third person fictional sentences, such as those with which *Anna Karenina* begins. Here, the audience are to pretend to themselves or make-believe that the sentence 'Everything was upset in the Oblonsky's house' is a true statement; they are to make-believe that there *was* an Oblonsky's house, and that everything *was* upset in it. Hence, in third person fictional sentences, the author's merely uttering the sentence normally makes it fictionally true. The only exception to this is when an author's sentences are inconsistent, as when he refers to a character once as twenty-one and once as twenty-two years old, without any lapse of fictional time (we shall return to this point when discussing fictional truth in Chapter 8.) We must then adapt our account of fiction to take note of this distinction, overlooked by many theorists, between first and third person fictional sentences.

Invented narratives

This is, however, to speak of fictional sentences only; and what we want to get at is fictional *discourses*, or *works* of fiction. Here another important feature of fiction (which, incidentally, also distinguishes it from irony) should come to our notice: *works* of fiction are all narratives. A necessary feature of a work of fiction is that it tells, or in the case of drama, presents, a story. This is the sense noted by the dictionary, that fiction is an 'invented narrative'.

What is it, though, for a discourse to tell a story, to be an invented narrative? There is no clear cut answer to this question. 'Story' and 'narrative' are words whose edges are blurred. This does not limit their usefulness, but it does frustrate misguided attempts to draw sharp boundaries round them. A narrative or story, not only in fiction, but also in such uses as 'the story of my early life', 'the story of the universe', 'the story of our nation', etc. are accounts (or dramatic presentations – I shall ignore this tiresome qualification from now on) of a sequence of (however loosely) connected events, characteristically involving persons, objects and institutions. Because of the blurry edges, it is impossible to say just how extensive a sequence must be in order to qualify as a story, though the longer and more connected it is, the more sure we may be that it is one. Nor is it possible to say what the subjects of stories must be. In fictional works, the stories usually concern persons (whether they themselves are fictional or not – Anna Karenina, or the emperor Hadrian), or quasi-persons (the Tin Man, the little blue engine). This feature, however, reflects the kinds of fictional stories or narratives we are most interested in, rather than the limits of possible story-telling or narratives. A story can be told about a fictional kettle or a blade of grass, where these are not treated as quasi-persons; but it would be unlikely to hold our interest long, and certainly not in the way a story or narrative about a fictional person or quasi-person might. This fact, incidentally, suggests one reason why fiction is important to us. As the Roman playwright Terence put it in 163 BC: 'I am a man; I hold nothing human foreign to me.'[12] Fiction standardly deals with human life under one aspect or another, and there are few of us who are not interested in that.

Fictional discourses and irony both involve make-believe or nondeceptive pretence. But the way in which pretence enters into each of them is different. The difference arises from the different aims which each has: irony to contrast how things are with how they should have been, or might have been expected to be; fiction to engage the audience in make-believe, in a nondeceptive pretending to themselves, to tell a tale, a story, to provide a narrative. This is not to deny, of course, that there may be ironical stories or narratives; it is only to say that ironical utterances are not *ipso facto* fictional; they need not constitute a story.

In explaining fictional discourse, we had to shift from discussing fictional sentences to discussing fictional works. I have suggested that, to determine whether a given utterance is a case of irony or fiction, we need to look at the aim with which, and the context in which, it was uttered. But that may seem to have left a thread about some types of sentences dangling untidily, a question unanswered. How, we might ask, are we to describe a one-sentence make-believe or nondeceptive pretended illocutionary act of stating when it is neither ironical nor fictional – or are there no such sentences? The answer is that it seems that indeed there are (one uttered in an acting class demonstration, for instance, might be one); but we must look at the aim with which, the context in which, the sentence is uttered in order to determine what acts their utterings constitute. If I nondeceptively pretend to state that you are early (by uttering the sentence 'You are early' without its standard illocutionary force), I may intend to draw attention to, and possibly rebuke, your actual lateness. In that case, as we have seen, the para-illocutionary act I perform is an ironical one. But I may utter the same sentence in order to perform a different para-illocutionary act: that of parodying an utterance of yours, for instance, or of giving a secret signal. Once we see that here, too, it is the aim with which, and the context in which, a sentence is uttered that determines how we are to classify it, this residual problem disappears. Nondeceptive pretended or make-believe illocutionary acts may be performed for a variety of reasons. One of them is to tell a story; others are not.

Invention and reality

A work of literary fiction is an invented narrative, consisting of sentences which the author invites the audience to make-believe are true, or to make-believe are authentic utterances of a real or imaginary utterer. We must say something more about the notion of invention that we have invoked here. I will speak only of fictional sentences now, but what I say about them will be true, *mutatis mutandis*, of narratives as well, and also of nonlinguistic forms of fiction-making. I shall speak, for the sake of simplicity, only of fictional sentences that the author invites the audience to make-believe are *true* (again, my remarks can be adapted easily enough to other kinds of fictional sentences).

A fictional sentence of this type is one which the author invites the audience to make-believe is true. But this is not enough; we need to add two other conditions. The first is that the sentence is one that he himself does not believe to be true. We need this condition to capture the notion of invention which is part of the notion of fiction. For the idea of invention employed here is that of *making something up* – authors of fictional sentences must have made up or invented their contents, the scenes and events they describe. They cannot, in the relevant sense, have made up the contents of a sentence if they simultaneously believe it is true. (People who are self-deluded may, of course, be told that they, or their imaginations, have 'made up' what they believe; but that is not the sense in which we speak of people intentionally making things up when they utter a fictional sentence. We shall return to this matter in Chapter 5.) So if a sentence is fictional, the author does not believe it is true.

Here is an illustration of this point. Suppose a nineteenth-century Russian mother uttered a sentence with the implied invitation to her children that they should make-believe it was true, and suppose it was a sentence which, though she did not assert it, she herself believed was true (or believed expressed a true proposition).[13] She might have announced, for instance, that she was going to tell the children a story, and gone on to utter the sentence 'Napoleon rode through the streets of Moscow bare-headed on the day he ordered his troops to withdraw'. She would not have *asserted* that Napoleon did that, she would have invited her audience to *make-believe* it. But she herself might have believed that Napoleon rode through the streets of Moscow bare-headed on that inauspicious day. Then she would not have uttered a fictional sentence, although she would have fulfilled the first condition of doing so, and although her audience might well believe she had done so; for, since she believed that what she was saying was true, it would not be something that she had made up or invented. That would be so even if in fact her belief was false and Napoleon did not ride bare-headed through the streets of Moscow on that day; people who have a false belief do not make it up – they are simply mistaken.

What we have just said should not be confused with the view that a fictional sentence cannot turn out to be true. For there is no incompatibility between a sentence's being 'made up' in the way we have explained and its being in fact true. Suppose, for example, that the author of the story beginning with the sentence mentioned above did not in fact believe that Napoleon rode bare-headed through the streets of Moscow on the day he ordered his troops to withdraw – suppose, in other words, that the sentence was a fictional one. Yet it might still turn out to be a true one as well. Subsequently discovered documents might show that is exactly what Napoleon did. That would not, however, show that the author had not, after all, produced a fictional sentence. Some fictional sentences might turn out to be coincidentally true in this way, and it is even conceivable that a whole fictional narrative might, too.

A possible case of a narrative's turning out to be true shows the need for the third condition which a sentence must satisfy in order to be a fictional sentence. The case is that of 'unconscious memory.' Suppose Virginia Woolf had produced a narrative which she believed herself to have invented, but which, it turned out later, was true of some of her own childhood experiences, although at the time of writing the narrative she had no conscious memory of them. Suppose, further, that it was those experiences that determined the content of the sentences in which she formulated her narrative. To give this bare suggestion some colour, we can suppose that the narrative was a short one about nineteenth-century London and that it began with a sentence describing Queen Victoria riding through the gates of Buckingham Palace in a black carriage accompanied by two of her ladies in waiting. We will suppose now that in fact, as a child, Woolf actually saw Queen Victoria exactly as the narrative's opening scene described her, but that she had since completely forgotten it – as far, at least, as her conscious memory went. Although she had no conscious memory of what she saw, however, it was the experience of seeing the old Queen that caused the thoughts and images which she expressed in the opening sentence of her narrative, and which she believed herself to have invented.

This imaginary case of unconscious recall suggests that, although she would not have believed her sentence to be true, Woolf would not have been inventing, or making up, its content in the way that fiction requires. Hence it seems we need to add a third condition to those we have already stated for a sentence to be fictional.[14] It is not easy to formulate this condition precisely without either letting in or keeping out too much. A faint echo of a past experience would surely not disqualify an author's sentences from being fictional, but requiring an exact match of detail before we disqualified them, supposing we could make sense of that idea, might exclude too much. Perhaps we should say that the contents of the author's sentence should not be preponderantly determined by unconscious recall, and acknowledge that there will be a blurry area where it will be uncertain whether this condition has been satisfied or not. Alternatively, we might say that if the fiction is true, it must be so only coincidentally; an unconscious memory will not be true coincidentally, but by virtue of a causal connection through memory to the events which produced the memory.

Both these formulations, suggested by Currie, have been challenged by Lamarque and Olsen on the ground that they are unnecessary. All we need to do, they argue, is to specify that the *content* of the putative fictional sentence must be fictional; and whether that is so will depend on whether it originates in a fictive utterance (i.e. one which the author invites the audience to make-believe is true) and on how it is described in that utterance.[15] Thus, presumably, since the origin of the content of Woolf's hypothetical sentence would not lie in the fictive utterance, and what is true of the content would not be 'determined by the way they are described' in the utterance, the sentence would not be fictional. But if Woolf had merely used her past experience, unconsciously recalled, and made something different out of it, then the sentence would have been fictional.

It is not easy to choose between these accounts of the third condition, and perhaps not important to do so here. What matters is that we recognise the need for it.

Fictional sentences of the type we have discussed, then, are sentences which the author invites the audience to make-believe are true, which the author himself does not believe are true, and the contents of which are not formed by direct unconscious recall. This account can be adapted quite easily to accommodate the other types of fictional sentences that it does not fit as it stands.

Nonliterary fiction

I said at the beginning of this chapter that not all fiction is literary. We have mime plays and wordless strip cartoons; and we may have paintings that represent a sequence of events involving imaginary characters and situations: Hogarth's *The Rake's Progress* series, for example. How are we to accommodate the account I have given of fictional discourse to works like these where, clearly, since there is no language, there can be no question of sentences, whether uttered as make-believe or pretended statements, etc., or as sentences which the author invites the audience to make-believe are (sometimes true) statements, etc.? The answer, I think, is quite simple. These representations of a series of imaginary events are the nonlinguistic counterparts of the utterances we make-believe are true, or make-believe are truly utterances in the case of literary fiction.

Consider the difference between a war artist's depiction of the progress of actual battle scenes, and the imaginary depictions which might be executed by a Goya. The war artist, in so far as he was representing what he saw, would be attempting to show how things were at a certain place at a certain time. This is analogous to a reporter's attempting to describe the same scene in words. Neither would be engaged in the production of a work of fiction (though both might, of course, distort the truth). The difference between the war artist and the reporter here is that the one *portrays* how things are, the other *states*. Portraying is analogous in the nonlinguistic, visual domain to stating in the linguistic domain. One may portray accurately, and one may state truly: the effect is the same – the audience acquires information about the subject of the portrayal or statement. (Many other things may also be happening to the audience in both cases; they may be emotionally involved, for instance, or impressed by the skill of the painter or reporter. But these things are not relevant here.) The difference between the war artist's representations and the imaginary ones of a Goya is analogous to that between the war correspondent's descriptions and a Hawthorne's or a Hemingway's. The 'Goya' paintings would be a series of portrayals we made-believe were accurate portrayals of actual scenes, just as the novelist's sentences, if in the third person, would be a series of utterances we made-believe were true descriptions of actual scenes. What made them fictional in each case would be the fact that the scenes were invented, not observed, and that the audience was invited to pretend to themselves that they were portrayals, or descriptions, of actual scenes.

There is another feature in the perception of paintings, and visual art generally, which may sometimes tend to obscure this truth, and may have led Walton, as we noticed at the beginning of this chapter, to think that all representational paintings are fictions. It is that when we look at a representational painting – whether of an imaginary or of an actual scene – we 'see' the paint daubs as, say, a field with a house and a tree in it. This 'seeing as' is a feature of our apprehension of the canvas, and, in some sense yet to be explained, involves our imagination. It is easy to conclude from this (as perhaps Walton did) that all representational paintings must therefore be in some way fictional – that we, as it were, make-believe we are looking at a field with a house and a tree in it, just as the reader of third person fiction makes-believe he is reading true statements. This is a mistake because the fact, if it is one (I shall return to this point in Chapter 5) that we make-believe the paint daubs are a field with a house and tree in it when we 'see' them as such, would not be enough to make the picture a work of fiction. When we look at the news pictures on our television screens, we may see the dots and lines as a field with a house and tree in it, but that does not make the news pictures fictions. Our picture-contemplation cannot be fiction-contemplation unless the scene depicted is imaginary – that is, invented; and even then, we would still need that central idea of fiction, that there is a story, a narrative, before us.

Conclusion

There are some problems about fiction – the ontological status of fictional objects, for instance (do Hamlet or Anna Karenina in some sense 'exist', since we can talk about them although they are not real?) – which I shall not discuss. They belong perhaps more to the study of metaphysics than to that of literature.[16] But there are other problems – about the way in which fiction may convey truths, for example, and about what is true in a work of fiction – which clearly do belong to the study of literature. I shall consider these in Chapter 8. The next topic, however, concerns a problem that concerns our *reaction* to works of fiction: how can we really be moved by the fate of fictional characters, if we know all along that they and all their doings and sufferings are only imaginary?

4

PSYCHOLOGICAL REACTIONS TO FICTION

Prologue

Works of fiction affect us profoundly. We are moved, amused and even frightened when we read, watch or contemplate them. Usually, our emotions are for the characters we encounter in the works. We pity Anna, in *Anna Karenina*, when she is deserted by Vronsky, and fear for her as, at the end, she walks towards the train; we are pleased for Elizabeth Bennett, in *Pride and Prejudice*, when she and Mr Darcy finally become engaged, and we feel terror for the victim as the murderer in Hitchcock's film *Rear Window* stalks his helpless prey. Sometimes, though, we are affected more directly. When, in a horror film, a monster or ghost appears to be looming towards us from the screen, we recoil in horror; and the reaction, although caused by a fictional character, is for ourselves, not for a character in the film. Nothing could be clearer than that works of fiction arouse emotions, or, more generally, psychological reactions, in us, and that it is fictional characters and events that are the objects or the source of those reactions.

Or so it seems. But, on reflection, we may wonder if this really can be so. To take the reaction of fear first (and some theorists have, to their cost, taken little else), it appears that perhaps we aren't *afraid* after all. For (it seems) there are three features characteristic of fear: belief that some real being is in danger; physiological sensations (quickened pulse, sweating palms, etc.), and the behavioural disposition to escape (or help the apparently threatened being escape) the danger. If we consider the characteristic of belief alone, surely, when I am reading a novel or watching a film or play about a fictionally endangered person, I do not believe I am reading about or watching any real endangered being. Watching *Rear Window*, I do not believe I am watching either a real person stalking another real person with murderous intent, or a historically accurate representation of such a person and such a stalking. Reading Tolstoy's account of Anna's approach to the train, I do not believe I am reading about the suicide of a real woman called Anna Karenina. How, then, can I really be experiencing fear? Or if, alternatively, I really am experiencing fear, must I not either have forgotten that nothing dangerous is really happening to any real person, in which case I am childishly deluded, or else simply be afraid where there is no cause for fear, in which case I am childishly irrational?

This problem has provoked a good deal of discussion among theorists, much of it, I believe, mistaken. The aim of this chapter is to correct the mistakes and thereby solve the problem. In doing so, we shall have to appeal implicitly to the concept of imagination, a key, but elusive concept, which we must, however, get some grip on if we are to think clearly about fiction and other aspects of literature.

Psychological reactions and belief

Suppose, on your entering a friend's room, she announces with tears in her eyes 'My brother has just been killed in a road accident'. Believing her, and knowing her brother well, you will naturally feel shock, sadness and sympathy. Suppose, however, that your friend smiles as you fumble for something to say, and says 'My brother is perfectly well and has not been in any accident – I am merely rehearsing my part in a play I am acting in'. Then, if you now believe her, since you no longer believe her brother has had an accident, you will normally cease to feel shocked, sad, or sympathetic, although you may well feel annoyed at the way you have been misled. Suppose, now, that you receive a phone message from your doctor that your latest test shows you have an incurable disease. Believing this, you will probably feel depressed and anxious. But suppose a moment later the doctor rings to say that you are perfectly healthy, and that your test result had been confused with someone else's. If you believe the doctor now, you will normally cease to be depressed and anxious, although you may well feel resentment about the confusion, and sympathy for the other person.

These thoughts suggest the following principle:

(P) A necessary condition of feeling sadness, sympathy, shock, fear, etc. is that you believe that something sad, bad, shocking, dangerous, etc. has happened, or is or may be going to happen, to some real person or thing.

(It is not clear how we should fill in the 'etc.' in (P). Many philosophers, I noted just now, are content to let fear and pity stand as representatives for all psychological reactions, and have not scrutinised a wider range of cases. This omission has, I think, led them astray. We shall look at other types of psychological reactions shortly, but for the time being, we can assume that

(P) is intended to range at least over the reactions actually mentioned.) Some philosophers, notably Kendall Walton,[1] apparently accept (P), although they might wish to qualify it with respect to fear, arguing that we can feel fear only where danger is expected or believed present, not also when it is believed to be past.[2] They conclude, therefore, that when we are 'saddened' by the death of Anna Karenina, or 'afraid' for the helpless prey in *Rear Window*, since we do not believe Anna or the victim are real persons, our 'sadness' and 'fear' are not real either. We are only 'quasi-sad' or 'quasi-afraid'. True, we may have the appropriate sensations – aching throats, pricking eyes, thudding hearts and sweating palms – but we do not have the appropriate *belief*. Nor, moreover, do we *behave* in the appropriate way. We do not, for instance, think of laying flowers on Anna's grave, or of summoning the police to help save the murderer's intended victim. Indeed, to take another example, not only do we not try to stop Othello from killing Desdemona, but we would be disappointed if, instead of doing so, he told her he now realised he had made a terrible mistake and begged her pardon. Only one of the characteristic features of sadness or fear is present, that of physiological sensations and feelings. Since the other two, belief in the reality of what is depicted, and engaging in the appropriate behaviour, are missing, these reactions, it is claimed, cannot be real fear or sadness.

Make-believe reactions

What is going on? According to this view, the audience of the book, film or play are 'making-believe', or pretending to themselves, that there is a real person (Anna Karenina, Desdemona) suffering or in danger. The book, film or play is a 'prop' for their make-believe. In the world of the work, it is *fictionally* true that there is a person called Anna Karenina, or a person called Desdemona, and fictionally true that they suffer the fate described or presented in the work. It is such fictional truths that 'prescribe' the form of our make-believing, or determine, in other words, what we are to make-believe. We then, engaging in the make-believe of the fictional world presented by the author, make-believe that we care for Anna Karenina and for Desdemona, and hence make-believe that we are afraid for or pity them. But it is only make-believe fear and make-believe sadness. We participate in the fictional world, but, inevitably, in that world everything, including our psychological reactions, is make-believe.

Why is it that making-believe, or pretending to yourself, that you are afraid or sad generates real sensations and feelings (your heart races, there is a weight on your chest, you feel tears in your eyes)? This theory cannot tell. It can say only: it may be strange, but there it is. Nor can it explain why it is that we often describe ourselves, after the book or episode is finished (and we are no longer making-believe), as having been saddened by Anna's fate or fearful for Desdemona. Why do we not say instead that we made-believe really well, or pretended to ourselves with gusto, that we felt sadness or fear? The theory does not tell us that, either.

Another question is sometimes asked, however, which the theory can answer. It is this. Are there not occasions when people, watching a play or film, or even, perhaps, reading or listening to a story, just 'forget themselves'? Or forget, rather, that it is only a work of fiction. Do not people sometimes temporarily believe they are watching, reading or hearing about real people and real events, not fictional ones? Surely children and people with powerful imaginations may quite easily slip into this state and, when they do, are they not experiencing real fear and real pity?

The answer is, of course, yes; but that does not mean the theory is wrong. For what the theory is concerned with is the reactions of people – 'normal' readers, listeners and viewers – who know all along (although they need not, and probably will not, be *telling* themselves all along) that it is fiction they are reading, listening to or viewing. It is such people's responses that we are trying to explain, not those of uninstructed children or deluded adults. For it is only the reactions of the normal member of the audience that give us a philosophical problem. There is no philosophical problem, but only an educational one, about people's forgetting that they are dealing with fiction. They are ignorant or deluded, and that, apart from instructing or undeceiving them, is all there is to it. The philosophical problem is to explain how people who are not deluded or ignorant can nevertheless apparently have real psychological reactions to fictional events, and the theory's answer is that they do not – they *make-believe* they have those reactions.

Some of those who maintain we are really fearful for Desdemona and really sad for Anna may be tempted to reject this disparagement of amnesia's role. Citing the fact that when we have been 'involved' in a novel or play or film, we may report this fact by saying that we 'forgot ourselves' while we were reading or watching it, these theorists may think that what happens in the readers' or viewers' minds is a continual fluctuation between forgetting that it is a fictional work they have to do with, and recollecting that, after all, it is a fictional work. We forget it long enough, the idea seems to be, to feel fear or sadness, but remember it in time to stop ourselves rushing off to summon the ambulance or the police; and then we forget it again. Recognising the occurrence of occasional amnesia, they may be tempted to elevate it to the status of a general explanation. Children and over-imaginative souls, they say, may forget, but they are not alone: so do normal readers and viewers; they alternately forget and remember that it is fiction they are dealing with. How else, they will inquire, can we explain the fact that we do feel real fear and real sadness?

This theory will not do. It is like saying that because measles brings out spots in people, if people have spots they must have measles. We should remember, in the first place, that 'forgetting oneself' usually refers in these contexts to one's forgetting the preoccupations of one's ordinary life, not to forgetting that the fictional characters and events that absorb one *are* fictional characters and events. But, in the second place, even if we take the latter interpretation of 'forgetting oneself', these theorists are doubly mistaken. No doubt, first, such forgetting may sometimes occur, but it is quite wrong to think that it always does so when we are experiencing psychological reactions to the characters and events of fictional works. Nor, second, is this the only way in which we could hope to justify the claim that our reactions are real, not make-believe ones.

On the first point, whether or not we accept the make-believe theory, we must, I think, agree that most sane, sensitive readers of *Anna Karenina* and viewers of *Othello* do not *forget* they are holding a work of fiction in their hands or sitting in the theatre watching a fictional play or film. They may be quite well aware that the light is fading, for instance, or that someone is eating popcorn in the next row, all the time that they are experiencing their psychological reactions, however we describe them, to what is going on in the novel, play or film. While recognition of such things may disturb their absorption, it does not recall them from obliviousness to recollection of the *fictionality* of what they are reading or viewing; they had not forgotten *that* at all. Hence they may feel fear for Desdemona, or pity for Anna, and simultaneously admire the skill of the actress playing Desdemona, or dislike the smallness of the print. What misleads those who are tempted to adopt this theory of general intermittent amnesia is the fact that, when reading a novel or watching a film or play with any degree of attention, we do not continuously have the thought before our minds that it is a work of fiction we are reading or watching. Hence, they conclude, we have forgotten that it is one. But the fact that we do not continuously have the thought that it is fiction no more shows we have forgotten that it is fiction than does the fact that we do not continuously have the thought that we are listening to a lecture show that we have forgotten we are listening to a lecture. To be aware that one is doing something is to be in some state or disposition with regard to it; but it is not to be in the state or manifesting the disposition of continuously thinking that one is doing it. When I was writing this sentence, I was aware that I was writing it; but I was not continuously thinking the thought 'I am writing this sentence' while I was writing it.

As to the second point, there are various ways in which we might hope to show that our reactions are genuine reactions; we shall see this shortly.

Alternative views

Some theorists reject (P). They are impressed by the reality of the sensations and feelings we experience while reading or viewing fictional works, and they say, therefore, that we do feel real sadness or fear. But they nevertheless accept a variant of (P). They say:

(P1) A necessary condition of feeling *rational* sadness, sympathy, shock, fear ... is that you believe that something sad, bad, shocking or dangerous ... has happened, or is or may be going to happen, to some real person or thing.

Hence, on their view, people who are 'saddened' by Anna Karenina's death, or who 'fear' for Desdemona, do feel real sadness and real fear, but they are being irrational.[3] For they feel real pity and fear for Anna and Desdemona, although they know full well there is no real Anna or Desdemona for them to feel pity or fear for.

Such accounts offer a solution to the original problem, but replace it with another, and one, moreover, for which it is usually claimed no solution can be found. We behave irrationally in these matters, proponents of these accounts suggest, and perhaps there is nothing we can do about that, except acknowledge it. This is hardly a satisfying conclusion, although that does not mean it is wrong.

Other theorists argue that it is not Anna Karenina, Desdemona, or the helpless prey in *Rear Window* we are upset about, although what happens to those fictional persons is what occasions our psychological reactions. It is real people in general that we are afraid or sorry for – people who we think do or might suffer fates similar to Anna's or Desdemona's.[4] This might be a satisfying account, for it preserves both the stubborn intuition that it is genuine emotion that we feel and the rationality of our doing so, but for the fact that it misrepresents the problem we originally stated. For, while it may be true that we think of real women in actual or possible distress when we read *Anna Karenina* or watch *Othello*, it certainly is not true that we think of them alone. It is also, and primarily, or, perhaps, sometimes only, Anna Karenina and Desdemona – the fictional characters – that we apparently feel pity or fear for. By denying or ignoring that, this theory parts company with the problem. It is our reaction to the *fictional* persons that we want to understand, and, whatever that reaction is, it cannot be explained by shifting our attention to a possible reaction to real persons.

Still other theorists, following some remarks of Coleridge's,[5] argue that in viewing or reading fictional works, we 'suspend our disbelief' in the reality of the fictional characters. When the disbelief is suspended, the claim would appear to be, our emotions can legitimately flow. For we are not then reacting, irrationally, to characters we believe are not real persons; that belief, having been suspended, is somehow decommissioned, and no longer engages with our emotional behaviour.

An advantage of this theory is that it acknowledges that it is for Anna and Desdemona that we feel sad or afraid; so it locates the problem where it actually lies. A disabling disadvantage is that the idea of suspension of disbelief, on which it so heavily relies, is left virtually unexplained, so that the theory is liable to crumble under the denseness of its own obscurity. Shall we think of a suspended disbelief as one we cease to be aware of? Then the theory collapses into the theory, already rejected as irrelevant, that we forget that Anna and Desdemona are not real people. Or shall we say that a suspended disbelief is one about the truth, or, rather, falsity, of which we are, or make ourselves, unsure (as when we 'suspend judgement' on some hypothesis)? Then the theory is the vastly implausible one that we don't quite know whether to think that Anna and Desdemona are real people or not – a state, in any case, requiring information or therapy rather than philosophical illumination. Or shall we say that, in suspending our disbelief, we merely treat the fictional characters, etc. *as if* they were real ones? That, we have argued, is true; but then we need an account of how treating the characters *as if* they were real enables us to have reactions that are not *as if* they were real pity and fear, etc., but *are* real pity and fear, etc. Without such an account, the theory merely presents a problem in place of a solution. But if, on the contrary, it is alleged that our reactions *are* 'as if' reactions, not real ones, the theory collapses into Walton's theory, which we have already seen we have some reason to doubt.

The belief criterion

We have several proposed solutions, none of which is wholly convincing, while some seem to be well off the mark. It is time to start again.

Sometimes we are prey to irrational fears or phobias. Some people, for instance, are terrified of flying, although they believe that flying is as safe as other modes of transport which they do not fear at all. They are aware of the statistics about the relative dangers of flying *vis-à-vis*, say, road travel, and believe those statistics when they appear to show that flying is as safe as, or even safer than, driving to one's destination by motor bike. Nevertheless, they will cheerfully drive their motor bike from London to Edinburgh rather than take the plane; indeed, when they have to board a plane, although they have not forgotten or lost their faith in the statistics, panic overwhelms them.

This phenomenon is an analogue of the phenomenon of what Aristotle called *akrasia*,[6] or 'weakness of will', much discussed by philosophers. In weakness of will, a person believes that, all things considered, a certain action is the one that, morally or prudentially, he ought to do, and yet he chooses not to do it. In one way, weakness of will is not a problem. We all seem to experience it at some time or another, so its existence can hardly be denied. But in another way, it is very puzzling. What explanation are we to give – in terms of what reasoning, or faults of reasoning or whatever else – of our knowingly choosing what we believe is not the best action for us to do? The phenomenon of irrational fear is similarly problematic. We know it occurs, but we do not fully understand how it occurs, how exactly the linkage between thought and action fails so that some people fear flying but not biking, while simultaneously believing that flying is no more, or even less, dangerous than biking. Another analogue is the phenomenon of self-deception. How can a politician both believe he is going to lose the election and simultaneously persuade himself that he is not?

Fortunately, we do not have to solve all these problems here. We have to notice only that there are irrational fears, as there is weakness of will and self-deception. Whatever the explanation of these phenomena is, as we shall see, it is not one that can be given for our psychological reactions to fiction. For whereas these phenomena are all in some way characteristically open to censure, or downright irrational, there is nothing censurable or irrational at all about our psychological reactions to fiction.

The existence of irrational fears does, however, suggest that (P) is wrong. For people with an acknowledged irrational fear of flying nevertheless also believe that flying is no more dangerous than other modes of transport that they (quite correctly) do not fear. Yet there is no doubt that they really do have a fear of flying. Irrational fears are one instance, of a psychological reaction without the alleged necessary condition of belief in the perilousness of what is feared, but there are many others.[7] If we now look at other examples, examples of fiction which philosophers have neglected, we will see there are many cases in which (P) seems false.

Let us start from the conclusion we have already reached about fiction: that, when reading or viewing fictional works, we are making-believe that the events and scenes and characters depicted are real. It does not follow, however, that we are also making-believe that our psychological reactions are real. Forget the staple examples of fear and pity on which theorists have almost exclusively ruminated, and consider humour first. When we watch or read a comedy, our reaction is to laugh, to be amused. When, in Charlie Chaplin's film *Modern Times*, Charlie seems to be caught up in the factory production line, and his head appears stuck between the cogs of a giant machine, our reaction is one of, sometimes helpless, amusement. When Lady Bracknell delivers one of her epigrams in Oscar Wilde's *The Importance Of Being Earnest*, we are, in a different way, equally amused. Yet there is no question of our believing that some real person is being or has been wrung through some real factory machine, or that some real person is delivering or has delivered a put-down to another real person. Amusement, it seems, is one psychological reaction that just does not require the belief condition stipulated in (P). We make-believe that the fictional characters and events are real no less in comedy than in tragedy, or in adventure, suspense or science fiction works; for they are all equally fictions. But there can surely be no question that we are experiencing real amusement and real delight at the fictional behaviour of the fictional characters. Our laughter is the laughter of real, not make-believe, amusement. Make-believe generates the psychological reaction of amusement, and the reaction it generates is not a make-believe, but a real one.

We do not have to go to literature or drama for such examples. When schoolchildren imagine (i.e. make-believe) their pompous head teacher has just slipped on a banana skin, they laugh. The mere thought of his doing so amuses them; what they feel is real, not make-believe, amusement, generated by a make-believe, not a real, banana-skin episode

Next consider the case of erotic literature. People who read an erotic book (say Pauline Réage's *The Story of O*)[8] know full well that O and all her adventures are fictional. They do not believe the particular sensual pleasures and pains the protagonist is represented as undergoing are the experiences of a real person called O, or, for that matter, of any other particular real person. But the readers do not fail for that reason to have the psychological reaction of desire and excitement aroused in them by what the fictional characters fictionally do and undergo – that, after all, is one of the aims of erotic literature, just as, according to the commonly accepted reading of Aristotle, the arousal of pity and fear is one of the aims of tragedy.[9] Engaged readers of erotic novels make-believe that real activities of real persons are being described in the book, but their psychological reactions to them are real, not make-believe, reactions.

These examples seem to constitute a very strong case for rejecting (P). Psychological reactions do not, apparently, in general require belief in the reality of what they are reactions to, and there seems no reason for regarding pity and fear as exceptions to this rule. It may well be that our reactions are often muted – our awareness that these are fictional goings-on may diminish the intensity of the emotion which the goings-on excite in us. But that does not mean that we are only making-believe that we feel them. We must now try to trace the consequences of this conclusion.

Psychological reactions without belief

(P) needs amending. We have to realise that fear and the other psychological reactions we have been considering do not require belief that the object or source of our reactions is a real person or thing, who or which really is or was in danger, abandoned, being ground through the cogs of a vast machine or putting-down other real persons. These reactions can occur, rather, when the subject of them either believes or makes-believe that such things are happening. (Instead of 'make-believe', I could have written 'imagine'; for it is to the concept of imagination that we are appealing when we speak of make-believe. But it is better to speak here in terms of the relatively clear concept of make-believe than in terms of the relatively murky and as yet unexamined concept of imagination.) Thus I can send a shiver of fear down my spine as I walk home late at night either by believing or by making-believe there is a mugger lurking in the shadows at the next corner. In the first case, I am committed to the truth of the proposition that there is a mugger there; in the second case, I am not – but, usually by producing vivid visual imagery, I make it seem to myself as if I were. That is real fear that I feel, although I do not believe there is a real mugger there, and do not run away or shout for help. Similarly, people imagining a pompous personage slipping on a banana skin do not believe he really is slipping on one, but their amused reaction is real, not make-believe, amusement. Involved readers of *The Story of O* do not believe they are reading about any real person called O who is enjoying or has enjoyed real sado-masochistic pleasures – they make-believe these things, although their reactions are reactions of real, not make-believe, pleasure. If their make-believe is vivid – which depends both on the author and on them – it *seems* to them as if they really are witnessing the scenes the novel portrays although they know they are not.

How does one contrive to seem to oneself to be, to have the illusion of, doing something while not believing that one is? The answer to this question cannot be given until we have investigated the concept of imagination more thoroughly (in the next chapter). But for the present, we can accept that it is possible, as these examples show, and wait till then to see how.

Let us now concentrate on fear for a while, to see how this revision of (P) will affect our analysis of that concept. We have seen that one may either believe or make-believe that someone is in danger, when one feels fear for that person. What else is required for fear? I believe that, with this, and another, minor, amendment the generally accepted account, or something like it, can stand. Ignoring their other uses, let us use the term 'conceiving' for both believing and making-believe, and 'conception' for belief and make-belief. According to this usage, someone who either believes or makes-believe or generally has the thought that something is the case conceives that it is so, or has the conception of its being so. Then we can say that fear is the characteristic sensations and feelings associated with the conception of someone as in danger, which together are apt to cause the subject to try to escape the danger conceived, or, if the danger is conceived as affecting another person, to help that person escape it. By 'apt' to cause such behaviour, I mean (borrowing the term from a theory in the philosophy of mind) that they *will* cause such behaviour in certain circumstances, but not necessarily in all – where escape is thought to be impossible or inappropriate, for instance, the behaviour may not occur.

What goes for fear will go also, *mutatis mutandis*, for all the other psychological reactions we have mentioned. We feel pity for someone if we have the characteristic sensations and feelings associated with the conception of that person as suffering which are together apt to cause us to try to help the person we think of as suffering. A pupil feels amused if he has the characteristic sensations and feelings of pleasure associated with the conception of a pompous head teacher slipping on a banana skin which together are apt to cause him to laugh or smile. In each case, the conception may be purely imaginative. We don't have to believe that anyone actually is endangered, suffering or banana-skinned, nor even that they may be. We merely have to conceive them, whether they are fictional or real people, as such. (Notice that this revision allows room for irrational fears like the fear of flying: the person who has an irrational fear of flying believes that flying is safe, but conceives of it, irrationally, as unsafe.)

Our reactions to fictional characters and events do seem, after all, to be real, not make-believe, reactions, and our account of the concepts of those reactions should be amended accordingly. But someone may object here that we are going too fast; for if it is real fear and real pity that we feel, the third, behavioural, feature that we mentioned earlier as characteristic of these reactions ought to come into play. Readers ought to behave towards Anna Karenina as they would towards a real, and fairly familiar, person whose abandonment and death they were reading about. Audiences ought to behave towards Desdemona as they would towards a real, fairly familiar, woman who they believed was about to be murdered by her jealous husband. But no one in their right mind would try to find out where Anna was buried in order to lay flowers on her grave, and no one in their right mind would try to stop Othello killing Desdemona. Only people for whom the distinction between reality and fiction has become blurred are tempted to undertake such absurdities. Even if we do have reason to surrender (P), it may be said, still our psychological reactions to fictional people and doings cannot be real reactions; for real reactions require the appropriate behaviour, and in these cases, in nondeluded people at least, the appropriate behaviour simply does not occur.

This objection is mistaken. We normally engage in the appropriate behaviour only when we think it right or possible to do so. To take a non-fictional case first, a man resigned to being shot tomorrow may feel fear, but if he either does not choose to escape or does not believe he can, it is only rational not to try. So if he is rational, he will not try; but that does not mean he does not feel real fear.

Turning now to fiction, since, if we are fairly rational, we are aware we cannot possibly affect the fictional characters or events we are reacting to – nor, moreover, would we want to affect them – we normally inhibit any inclination to engage in behaviour the purpose of which would be to affect them. So the fact that we don't engage in such behaviour shows we are rational, not that we are not really feeling pity, fear or amusement for the fictional characters we are reading about or viewing. It was for this reason that I suggested that, in characterising these reactions, we should say that they are apt to cause, not that they invariably do cause, the appropriate behaviour. We feel pity for Anna Karenina, and fear for Desdemona, but we no more seek to lay flowers on Anna's grave or attempt to rescue Desdemona than we seek to lay flowers on the grave of a real person whose body we believe does not have a grave, or attempt to save a real person whom we believe has already been killed. In both cases we know full well that, albeit for different reasons, we could not succeed. In the first case it is logically impossible, in the second, physically. We can, of course, stop reading or watching the novel or play, just as we can stop reading or watching a news report of yesterday's events or a history of events that took place a millenium ago. But in neither case does that prevent the occurrence of the fictional or factual events in their respective domains. What our action may prevent is not the end of the story, but our knowing the end of the story. It is for this reason that the yokel who is supposed to have leapt onto the stage to save Desdemona was behaving absurdly. He could not save Desdemona; he could only interrupt the performance. Once the play is written, Desdemona still dies in it, no matter how often the performance is interrupted. He might as well have tried to erase the last movement of a sonata by shooting the pianist, or prevent yesterday's murder by burning today's newspaper report of it.

Rationality: the point of it all

There is then no barrier at all to the view that our psychological reactions to fiction are real reactions. But this may seem to leave us with another problem: if they are real reactions must they not be irrational? Is it not irrational to feel sorry for Anna Karenina or fear for Desdemona, when we do not believe that they are real persons really suffering or in real danger? Is not that what distinguishes our reactions from the reactions we have towards those we believe are real persons, even when, because of physical impossibility, we cannot sensibly try to help them – we do believe they are, or were, suffering or in danger? By acquitting ourselves of the charge that our reactions aren't real reactions, haven't we condemned ourselves to confessing they are irrational? This is, of course, the conclusion reached by those whose views I mentioned earlier, those who reject (P), but replace it with (P1).

No, we are not behaving irrationally. When we understand why, we will become a little clearer about the roles that fiction can play in our lives.

Let us return to the example we used some time ago, of someone apparently telling us that her brother had just died. If we believed that she had never had a brother, it would be irrational of us to feel sorry for her (at least on that account). Yet, unless entangled in a theory, we would not think it at all irrational of someone to feel sorry for Desdemona or Anna Karenina as they face their fictional deaths. On the contrary, we would probably regard someone who was utterly unmoved by them as emotionally or aesthetically defective. Moreover, while we might be relieved that some real person whom we previously believed to have been killed turned out not to have been harmed at all, we might well feel disappointed – cheated, even – if Anna were to change her mind, or if Desdemona were to escape by hiding under the bed. We would feel that *Anna Karenina* had been turned into a novelette and *Othello* into a farce. What is the explanation, and, more importantly, what is the justification, of these different attitudes?

The first thing to observe here is that, in the nonfictional case, we could not give a reason for feeling sorrow; the emotion would be rationally unmotivated. But in the fictional case, we would be able to explain and justify our reaction by appealing to the (fictional) fact that Anna and Desdemona were suffering or in danger. This is, indeed, a difference, but it does not of itself get us out of our difficulty. Someone might say: 'I can see that nothing bad is fictionally happening to Iago or Vronsky at that point in the play, whereas it is to Desdemona and Anna. But that doesn't justify you in feeling sad for the two women. For although something bad is *fictionally* happening to them, still it is *only* fictional that it is happening at all, and it is simply irrational to get upset about something you don't believe has really happened or is really happening or is (or may be) really going to happen.'

Notice how absurd this objection would become if it were applied to the reaction of amusement, rather than to that of pity or fear. No one, I surmise, has ever suggested that it is irrational to feel amusement at the representation of a pompous personage slipping on a banana skin, when we know full well that his doing so is a fictional occurrence in a comedy, and that no real pompous person is undergoing any such upheaval. It is, apparently, only our reactions to 'negative' fictional events (those that arouse such emotions as pity and fear) that the theorist castigates as irrational. There is a reason for this partiality, of course: pity and fear are emotions we would normally prefer not to feel – or, more accurately, would prefer not to have occasion to feel. Men seek happiness, and, whereas amusing things might be thought to be constituents of that happiness, it is hard to see how sad and fearful things could be so. In paradise, it is said, there is no suffering (although, admittedly, it is rarely said that there is laughter). We shall return to this theme in a moment. For the time being, however, let us take up the theorist's objection that the emotions of pity and fear towards occurrences we believe to be fictional are as irrational as they would be if they were directed towards similar nonfictional occurrences we believed had not occurred, were not occurring or were not going to occur.

It is important to remember that it is in the telling of the story or the playing of the play that our emotion is generated. If the author and, in a drama, the actors, director, stage designer, etc. have all been successful, and if we ourselves have participated fully in the make-believe, we are deeply interested in what is going to happen, in the fate of the characters who we make-believe are real people. A mere recital of the outline of the plot would not cause the reaction that we feel when we are reading the novel or watching the play, any more than the bald report of the result of a tennis match would normally cause the excitement, tension, elation or disappointment that watching it would cause in an involved spectator. It is by imagining, or making-believe, the whole detailed world of the fiction that we

65

come to be concerned for the fate of the characters in that world. (In this respect, fiction is no different from fact. A brief report of Caesar's assassination would not normally affect us as much as a full account of it in a detailed biography; and a summary of Shakespeare's *Julius Caesar* would hardly affect us as much as a performance of it.) It is the story or play that we want to hear or see, and the pity and fear are consequences involved in our seeing or hearing it.

The answer to the charge that we are being irrational in reacting as we do to the fictional events of *Anna Karenina* or *Othello* is that the emotions generated by Anna's and Desdemona's fates are emotions generated by integral features of an activity of make-believe that we value and choose to engage in. They are thus emotions which, like the activity which generates them, serve a purpose in our lives. That is what distinguishes them from a reaction of pity expended on the 'death' of our friend's nonexistent brother; that would be a reaction we would not normally choose to have, and one which, playing no useful role in our lives, would be absurd and wasted if we did. Our emotion in the fictional case, in other words, is rational because, in the imaginative or make-believe circumstances in which it is grounded, it satisfies our desires or needs, whereas in the nonfictional case of our friend's nonexistent brother's 'death' it would not normally satisfy any, or at any rate any rational, desire or need.

What are the desires or needs which the make-believe, and its attendant reactions, serve? Why are we so interested in, fascinated by, these fictions, this make-believe? I do not know if there is a complete answer to this question, for our interests and our needs are manifold, and probably mutable as well. But we can, at least, suggest some of the main reasons for our interest, reasons that are likely to be general, if not universal. First, just as we are fascinated by the lives of interesting real people whom we have never met – removed from us by time and space – so we may be equally fascinated by the lives of fictional people. For these do not show us, as history does, merely how things are or were in fact; they suggest how things might be. Not only is that interesting in itself; it also offers us reflective perspectives upon how things are with us. Second, there is also an element present in many forms of imaginative play, from childhood on, of rehearsal, of dealing vicariously in our imaginings with situations which concern us, and which are of a type we more or less dimly apprehend we may one day face. We play them out in preparation for the real thing, just as lion cubs in play are rehearsing for the hunt that will enable them to survive, or pilots rehearsing in the simulator emergencies they may one day have to deal with. It is partly because of our sense of our own possible destinies and misfortunes that we find those of Anna and Desdemona, of Hamlet and Othello, so gripping. Third, there is the fact that our actual lives are usually relatively narrow and confined, both in scope and quality. Contemplating other lives, albeit in make-believe, can be consoling or enriching, even when those other, fictional, lives, as do our own, involve suffering and danger. For it is the lives in which the suffering and danger occur that interest us, not just the suffering and the danger in themselves.

These reasons, I am fairly sure, are as incomplete as they are incompletely described. There are, almost certainly, other and perhaps deeper longings which the fictions that arouse such emotions satisfy, quite apart from our enjoyment of the skill with which they are constructed (a feature I have deliberately omitted from this discussion). Perhaps Aristotle's cryptically brief pronouncements on catharsis[10] allude to one such need. Perhaps we need to purify our emotions, or purge them; or to work them out or off. But the reasons we have, however cursorily, discussed do explain why it is that our reactions to fiction are not irrational reactions. They also help us to explain three other otherwise puzzling matters.

The first is that, as we noted earlier, we accept in fiction emotions of pity, fear, etc., which in ordinary life we would normally prefer not to feel. We can readily understand why we want to be amused, whether by make-believe or real events; but why do we seek to engage in make-believe activities which we know will make us sad or scared? The explanation is that if our interest in fiction is partly (whether for recognition or forewarning) in make-believe that simulates something of the misfortunes that it is our destiny to face, we shall naturally want the make-believe in which such misfortune is depicted to contain elements which are fearful, pitiful, etc. We do not imaginatively confront those misfortunes by make-believe in which they do not occur.

The second, related, puzzle is that we would feel cheated if Desdemona escaped her fate by hiding under the bed, or Anna evaded hers by throwing her hat instead of herself beneath the train – although we should be relieved if that were to happen in reality. Quite apart from the jolt which the implausibility of such a turn in either work would give us, the explanation here, too, is that the desire to confront such misfortune in make-believe would be frustrated, if in the make-believe it did not happen. We resent the cop-out because it denies us something that we seek, and it is rational for us to seek, from such works.

The final puzzle, which the reasons given to explain the rationality of our psychological reactions may also solve, arises from the fact that we sometimes return to the same work again and again. The first time we may not know what is going to happen but in successive readings or viewings we not only know, but even eagerly anticipate, what will happen in the next scene or on the next page. Why do we seek to repeat the experience, particularly when we can only be less and less surprised by it? The explanation lies, again, in the needs such fictions satisfy. In make-believe, it is the experience of the activity that counts, not just its novelty; we return to it because we need to repeat the experience. Just as pilots need to return to their simulators and lion cubs to their play, so we too sometimes need to return to those make-believe activities in which our thoughts and feelings may be so much more variously and deeply engaged.

Conclusion

Our psychological reactions to works of fiction are real, then, but they are not irrational. In explaining why, I had recourse to two notions: make-believe (or pretending to oneself) and imagination. These are clearly related. It is time now to consider how.

5

IMAGINATION

Prologue

Fiction involves nondeceptive pretending to oneself, or make-believe. Our responses to fictional beings and events are responses to make-believe beings and events. Make-believe beings and events are imaginary; in both their creation and their apprehension our imaginations are at work. But imagination extends over many other activities as well. Indeed, for much of our life, from childhood to death, we are engaged in imagining in one way or another; there is hardly a more pervasive feature of mental existence than imagining. We would like to be able to say what imagining is. What is its nature and scope? What is its peculiar role in literature? The single most illuminating concept in terms of which we can explain imagination is that of make-believe.[1] But imagination is a Protean notion, and the concept of make-believe by itself will not explain all its various forms.

Forms of imagining

Let us begin by considering this variety. Some cases of imagining are cases of supposing, assuming or being inclined to believe. If Tim, when asked, 'Is Leila still at home?' replies, 'Well, she was half a minute ago, so I imagine she is now,' he is using 'imagine' in this sense, and his imagining is a case of supposing, assuming or tentatively believing. Another type of imagining consists in having a false belief or delusion. If Jack goes mad, and Jill tells the doctor, 'He imagines he's Napoleon,' she is attributing a false belief or delusion to him. The same type of imagining is invoked when Jill tells Jack, now suffering from hallucinations, that the Cossacks he sees are only imaginary. While these types of imagining are related to the imagining involved in literature, they are not themselves, except in morbid cases, that type of imagining.

A type that comes closer is the kind of imagining involved when we 'suppose' something in another sense from that just mentioned. If I ask you to suppose that Cleopatra's nose had been half an inch longer, I am asking you, not to assume it was half an inch longer or tentatively believe it was, but to *pretend to yourself* that it was. Suppose now you are asked to imagine how different the history of the world might have been if only Cleopatra's nose had been half an inch longer. This type of imagining consists in thinking of the probable consequences of a proposition hypothetically supposed (imagined) to be true (which shows, incidentally, that imagination should not be contrasted with reason: imagining often is a kind of reasoning). This activity qualifies as imagining because the reasoner does not believe the consequences did happen, but only that they might or would have happened if the supposition made had been true.

Next there is a group of activities and dispositions that constitute the type of imagining we are now principally interested in. These are activities like visualising a scene (Carol picturing Laurence in his office), hearing a tune in one's head (Michael 'hearing' the Moonlight Sonata as he thinks of his new compact disc), day-dreaming or making-believe (Eric drifting off on a stream of pleasant thoughts about Carol; Rupert and Holly playing cops and robbers; Joe making-believe he's been awarded the Nobel Prize for physics), and simply dreaming (Colin dreaming he is falling). These activities can be more or less complex, more or less coherent, more or less vivid and engrossing, more or less exciting or disturbing, saddening or amusing. Some of them can go on for a long time, be interrupted and resumed, be taking place while we are doing something else (walking, cleaning the windows, driving to work), and more or less deliberate or voluntary. Moreover, they may involve occurrent experiences (such as actually picturing Anna Karenina as we read Tolstoy's words 'Quickly and lightly descending the steps that led from the water tank to the rails, she stopped close to the passing train'[2]) or dispositions (such as having a sympathetic attitude towards Anna even while we are actually picturing, not her, but Vronsky 'walking up and down like an animal in a cage'[3]). It is to this group that much of the complex and structured imagining involved in reading a story or watching a play or film belongs. We shall look at it more closely in a little while, but first we should try to see if there is any common thread that runs through all these forms of imagining.

Imagination and reality

One thing we can say straight away is that, despite the etymology of the word (*imago*, an image or picture) imagining need not involve having mental images (whatever account we may give of what that consists in). The historian who imagines how history might have been different if Cleopatra's nose had been half an inch longer, and the children who make-believe they are cops and robbers need not be forming mental images all or any of the time they are so engaged, although they may well be, and probably are, sometimes actually doing so.

Roger Scruton has claimed that a, or perhaps the, common element in all forms of imagining is that 'imagination involves thought that is unasserted';[4] that is, to imagine is to think of propositions without asserting them. At the same time, imagining is also thinking of those propositions as 'appropriate'. On this account, to imagine the chairman as an elephant is to think the proposition that he is one, without actually asserting it, and to think that the description 'elephant' is appropriate to the chairman. Scruton excludes from his account varieties of imagining such as deluded belief, which clearly would not involve *unasserted* thought. When Jack deludedly imagines he is Napoleon, he does assert, when asked, the proposition that he is Napoleon. So this alleged common element is not present in all forms of imagining. However, even on its own terms the theory seems to be mistaken. It is not true of nondeluded forms of imagining that, even if it does involve unasserted thought, it necessarily involves thinking of a proposition as appropriate. We may very well imagine something to be the case without thinking the description of its being so appropriate. Tell me to imagine the chairman as an elephant, and I may succeed in doing so, 'seeing' him trumpeting wild commands as he waves his trunk about over his desk. But, as his loyal secretary, I may think the description wholly *inappropriate*. What I do in such a case is, not think the proposition appropriate, but *make-believe* that it is true, regardless of whether or not I think it appropriate.

This proposal does not help us. But there is something else that runs through all the manifestations of imagining we have mentioned. I will put it very vaguely at first: a contrast with reality. The contrast may be minimal as when, in my first example, Tim says he imagines Leila is still at home. By using the word 'imagine' he indicates a certain lack of commitment; an inclination to believe, perhaps, or a tentative belief itself – but one that he acknowledges by using 'imagine' may not be true, may not conform with reality. Tim, in other words, is allowing that he does not know, he is not certain, that Leila is still at home. Beliefs can be strong or weak; when they are prefaced by 'I imagine,' their weakness, the possibility of their not conforming with reality, is implicitly declared.[5] The contrast with reality in cases of false belief or delusion is, of course, obvious. When Jill says Jack imagines he is Napoleon, or imagines there are Cossacks in the garden, she indicates his beliefs are false, the Cossacks imaginary; that is, not real.

When we turn to imagining a different history for the world, the contrast is, in its way, just as obvious. What the historian imagines is something he does not believe really happened – propositions he does not believe are true. Visualising, daydreaming and making-believe all involve a version of the same pervasive contrast. If Carol visualises (imagines herself seeing) Laurence in his office, she does not believe she is actually observing him there; if Michael nondelusively imagines he is listening to the Moonlight Sonata, he does not believe he really is listening to it, and if Holly makes-believe Rupert is a robber, she does not believe he really is one.

71

The ways in which this thread of a contrast with reality manifests itself in different contexts are of course different from each other; but they are still as much manifestations of the same thread as are the various appearances of a stream in one place or another still manifestations of the same stream. They have, to invoke the theory we have cited before, a 'family resemblance'. Let us now try to give a more precise formulation to this rather vague notion of a contrast with reality. Let us say that whenever anyone imagines anything, either what he imagines is not so, although it seems to him that it is (delusions, dreams and false beliefs), or he does not fully believe (is not certain) it is so (Tim's imagining that Leila is still at home), or he disbelieves it is so (Michael's imagining he is listening to the Moonlight Sonata). That is why Carol cannot visualise (imagine) herself watching Laurence sign a letter in his office if she believes she is watching Laurence signing a letter in his office. The barrier is semantic, not psychological. It is not that Carol lacks some mental resource or other, but that we do not count someone as visualising something if she believes that she is actually watching it. Visualising is to be *contrasted* with believing you are watching, not associated with it. Hence, for the same reason, we do not count someone as pretending to himself, or making-believe, he is a Nobel Prize winner, if he believes he is a Nobel Prize winner.

A contrast with reality seems to be present in all forms of imagining, although it is not always the same contrast. Notice that we have not said it is only when someone is acting voluntarily (making-believe, or pretending to himself) that he disbelieves in the truth or reality of what he imagines. It is true that the dreamer and the hallucinator, who do not voluntarily imagine that they are falling or there are Cossacks in the garden, do not disbelieve they are falling or disbelieve there are Cossacks in the garden, either. But that does not mean that we can disbelieve in the truth or reality of what we imagine only if our imagining is voluntary. There are cases in which our imaginings are not voluntary, yet we disbelieve in the truth or reality of what we imagine. This is a point of some importance, which we shall return to shortly.

This conclusion, that imagining involves some contrast with reality, rests on an analysis of the uses of the word 'imagine' and its cognates. So it rests ultimately on the linguistic intuitions of competent speakers of English (and of other languages into which English can be translated). It is also a conclusion which some theorists have denied. Kendall Walton, for instance, holds: 'To say that someone imagines such and such is sometimes to *imply* or *suggest* that it is not true or that the imaginer disbelieves it. Nevertheless, imagining something is entirely compatible with knowing it to be true.'[6] His example of this alleged compatibility cites Fred, an imaginary shoe salesman, who daydreams that he wins a lottery and retires to the south of France. 'Much of what Fred imagines,' Walton claims, 'is false, and known by him to be false. But he imagines also that his name is Fred ... that France is in Europe, and much else that he knows to be true.'[7]

This is a mistake. To say that someone imagines something, in this context, is not to imply or suggest, but partly to state, that the imaginer believes that what he imagines to be so is not in fact so. This, I said, was a semantic feature of 'imagine' and its cognates. Just as many sentences in a work of fiction may be nonfictional statements of fact, so many features of a daydream may be nonimaginary features of the dream. When Conan Doyle writes that Sherlock Holmes lived in Baker Street, it is not Baker Street, but Sherlock Holmes and his living there that are fictional in the story. When Fred imagines himself winning a lottery and retiring to the south of France, it is not himself and the south of France that he imagines, but his winning a lottery and retiring there. This should not surprise us; Fred is telling himself a story, while Conan Doyle is telling others. That is the only significant difference, in this respect, between them.[8]

Imagination and make-believe

Fictional works are works of make-believe, and when we read or watch them we make-believe the fictional events and persons we read about, and the actors or images we watch, are real events and real persons. Or, where the persons portrayed are real, not fictional, persons, we make-believe that they did and underwent the things attributed to them in the fiction, and that, so far as drama is concerned, the actors portraying them are those persons. The authors (and directors, photographers, stage-designers and actors) induce, and to a large extent control, the imagining activities of their audience, who for their part co-operate with them. We imagine Anna as looking, saying, thinking or acting thus or thus, because that is how Tolstoy presents her to us; more precisely, it is what his words at once prescribe and typically cause us to imagine. In daydreams, much of our make-believe is under our control alone; in dreams, we do not make-believe at all – we are made to believe, and have no (at least, no conscious) choice over how our imaginings will go. In apprehending works of fiction we are somewhere in between. Our imaginings are prescribed and caused by others, yet there is scope for our own elaborations. No two readers, perhaps, imagine Anna exactly alike, and neither need be mistaken. But they are not at liberty to imagine her as dumb, unmarried or a resident of Monaco; Tolstoy's words exclude those possibilities. If readers do so imagine her, they misinterpret *Anna Karenina*, or step outside the make-believe of the fiction that Tolstoy composed. But what exactly is this imagining that is prescribed to the reader and which the author's words and, in dramatic fictions, the stage designer, cameramen, director and actors, typically cause the reader to experience?

Voluntary imagining begins with pretending to oneself or making-believe, involuntary imagining does not. What are voluntary and involuntary imaginings? Voluntary imaginings are not necessarily deliberately undertaken, but they are under our control in the sense that it is we who determine how they shall go. Eric, thinking of Carol, may 'drift off' into a daydream about her. He does not do so deliberately, but if the course and content of his daydream is determined by his own conscious choices, his imagining is voluntary. If, however, he opens a novel, while he may do so deliberately, the main course and content of his imaginings are determined, not by him, but by the author of the novel. In that sense, his imaginings are involuntary. When we imagine voluntarily, as in a daydream, we pretend to ourselves, or make-believe, that we are doing something that we disbelieve we are doing; we induce the illusion in ourselves that we are doing it. When we imagine involuntarily (in the sense just defined), we may undergo the illusion without ourselves directly causing the illusion to occur. The cause is, in literature, the author (director, actors, stage and camera crew, etc.) who, generally with our acquiescence, induce in us the illusion that we are doing or undergoing what in fact we believe we are not doing or undergoing. It is now time to take up my earlier observation (p. 62) that we may undergo an illusion, and frequently do, while knowing all along that it is an illusion. For recognition of this fact is the key to understanding this kind of imagining.

What is it to make-believe or pretend to oneself? We can answer this question most easily by asking a prior one: What is it to pretend? Let us start with pretending to perform an overt (i.e. publicly observable) action. This is intentionally to try to make it seem as though one is performing an action which one is not in fact performing by performing some, but not all, of the movements constituting that action. If Chad pretends to speak to Joyce, he typically opens and closes his mouth, and perhaps makes sounds, without issuing words. If Jill pretends to slap Jack, she typically swings her hand in the region of his face without striking him. In each case, the pretender performs some of the physical movements which constitute performing the action, without performing all of them; Chad makes no verbal sound, Jill no stinging contact with Jack's cheek. (If something goes wrong, and Chad does accidentally utter words, or Jill's hand does accidentally make stinging contact with Jack's cheek, they accidentally perform the action which they intended to pretend to perform. The action is accidental because there was no intention to perform it – indeed, an intention not to perform it.)

Second, when we consider moods and emotions, we can give a similar account. If someone pretends to be in some emotional state, he performs movements characteristically expressive of that state, but without having the relevant feelings. If Eric pretends to be angry, he shouts, thumps the table, or performs other acts from the repertoire of anger-expressing behaviour, without in fact feeling indignant. If Laurence pretends to feel sorry for Chad, he may pull a long face, and even make himself cry, but he feels no sorrow (or none, anyway, for Chad).

These are both types of pretence in which what we pretend is, or involves, physical movements. The pretence consists in making it seem that one is doing or feeling something either by performing some of the appropriate movements without performing all of them, or by performing appropriate movements without having the associated feelings. But merely imagining that one is doing or feeling something need involve no physical movements at all; how can we explain that in terms of pretence? If Alan imagines he is listening to Mark speaking Cantonese, there simply are no characteristic movements he need partially (or wholly) perform while not having the appropriate experience. He need not cup his ear, for instance, or screw up his face in an agony of quasi-concentration. When Michael 'hears' a tune in his head, his overt behaviour may be the same as when he hears no sound at all. It seems, at first sight, as though the notion of pretence is irrelevant here; how can it possibly illuminate what is going on in the case of imagining?

The answer is that in this kind of imagining we are not pretending to others, but making-believe, or *pretending to ourselves*. Alan pretends to himself, or makes-believe, that he is listening to Mark speaking Cantonese, Michael makes-believe, or pretends to himself, that he hears a tune. Pretending to oneself ranges over a spectrum from merely supposing or assuming to bringing it about that one seems to oneself to be, has the illusion that one is, doing or undergoing something while all the time believing that in fact one is not. Michael brings it about, by thinking of himself as listening to a tune, that he seems to himself to be actually doing so, although he does not believe that he actually is and actually believes he is not. Alan brings it about, by thinking of himself as listening to Mark speaking Cantonese, that he seems to himself actually to be listening to Mark speaking Cantonese, although he actually believes he is not.

It may be wondered how one can have an illusion and simultaneously believe it is an illusion. (This is the point I said was the key to understanding this type of imagination.) In one sense of 'illusion', of course, one cannot – the sense in which to have an illusion is to have a mistaken belief. Jack, when he is deluded or hallucinating, may be said to have an illusion in this sense; so, perhaps, may Eric, when he dreams. But there is another, and possibly more accurate, sense of 'illusion', according to which one can very well have an illusion and simultaneously believe it is an illusion, believe that what one seems to experience is not really so. Consider cases of mirages and *trompe l'oeil* paintings. Consider the hackneyed example of a straight stick half-immersed in a glass of water, or the Müller-Lyer diagram (see below).

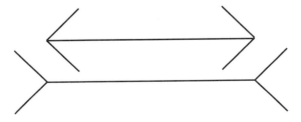

In all these familiar cases of illusion, we may, and generally do, know that things are not really as they seem – but they still *seem*. The stick we believe is straight, looks bent in the glass of water; the lines we believe are of equal length, look unequal; what we believe is only a shimmering haze on the horizon, looks like an oasis; what we believe are only painted figures, look like real people.

So it is with the picturing, visualising and similar types of imagining that we are considering here. The difference is that in voluntary imagining, we induce the illusion ourselves by our own thoughts and actions, whereas in the cases of the involuntary imagining and the illusions just mentioned, while we may submit to them willingly, the illusion itself is not induced by our own thoughts or actions. But that difference makes no difference here.

I said earlier that merely imagining need not involve physical movements. It is important to recognise that nevertheless it may and often does do so. In fact, much of our imagining, our making-believe or pretending to ourselves, involves overt physical movements. People who imagine themselves delivering a crushing retort to a loathed opponent in a debate are not likely merely to seem to themselves to be uttering the words and watching their opponent cringe; they are also likely to whisper the words to themselves, to adopt the sneer of cold contempt they imagine their faces wearing. When Michael 'hears' a tune in his head, he may well be beating time with his hand or even singing half-aloud. In these cases, making-believe or pretending to oneself resembles pretending to others; the pretenders perform some of the movements they might perform if they really were delivering a retort or listening to a melody.

Pretending to oneself is like pretending to others in another way, too. Just as Jill's pretending to slap Jack involves performing some, but not all, of the movements which constitute really slapping him, so her (vividly) pretending to herself that she is slapping him involves inducing some, but not all, of the mental features characteristically present when really slapping someone. She has the impression of swinging her hand, feeling the stinging impact, hearing the satisfying smack of palm on cheek, but she does not *believe* she is really swinging her hand, feeling the impact, hearing the satisfying smack, as she may when she is really slapping him – those mental features are absent. The more vividly she imagines, the more successfully she pretends to herself, the more, and the more completely, mental features of really slapping will be present; but belief, of course – so long as she is still only pretending to herself, only making-believe – will always be absent.

Imagination and literature

There are senses of 'imagination' and its cognates which are relevant to literature, but which we have not considered yet. An *imaginative* scientist or chess player is one who is highly *original*, who invents significant new theories or new moves. Fiction is often described as imaginative literature for the same reason – the author is original, he invents characters and events. Imaginative uses of language are those which create significant new styles, meanings or suggestions. (The contrast with reality which we noted earlier is still invoked in these senses, albeit distantly: the imaginative scientist, chess player or writer invents new theories or moves, has thoughts that did not exist – were not constituents of reality – before.) But I have nothing to say about this kind of imagination, apart from noting its existence, because there does not seem to be anything useful that can be said. Nearly all of us have some capacity to invent in this way, and gifted people (for once, the adjective is accurate) have it to a high degree. It is exercised in the *composition* of literature, and often part of what we admire. But it is not normally exercised to a high degree in the *apprehension* of literature. It is the role of imagination in our everyday apprehension of literature – especially 'imaginative' literature – that I want to examine more fully in this section.

However, we should remember that it is not only in the apprehension of fiction that our imagination is involved. The reading or hearing of any narrative, fictional or not (a newspaper report, for instance) will often also involve it. The sentences we read or hear do not just impart propositions to us; they also cause us to 'picture', to 'hear' and 'feel' in our own way much of what they describe. Fiction imparts propositions to us that we make-believe or pretend to ourselves describe the deeds and sufferings, or are the utterances, of actual people, and the author's sentences often cause us to imagine (to picture) the events and characters fictionally presented to us. But the same sentences, if they were not fiction but factual assertions, could cause us to picture (to 'see', 'hear' and 'feel') in exactly the same way. The difference between fiction and nonfiction, in this respect, is that one of the chief points of fiction is to cause this imagining, but not to cause belief in the reality of what is imagined, whereas the chief point of nonfiction is to produce belief, whether or not it also causes this imagining.

Take the following passage, for example:

> Then suddenly a strange thing happened. The beam of the search-light on top of the water tower collided with another light, the yellow ray of the enemy searchlight.
>
> The two powerful lamps pointed their jets of light straight at each other's eyes, as if trying to dazzle the other to death.
>
> Opposite loomed the disjointed forms of the mountains, lit by a garish reddish-purple glow.
>
> The two beams of light remained locked in a furious embrace, piercing each other's eyes, bitter and stubborn, like knives poised for murder or like drunken lovers.[9]

If the writer's sentences engage our imagination, which is partly, of course, a matter of our own interests and capacities as well as his, we may imagine, in the sense of 'picture' or visualise, a variety of things. We may picture beams of brilliant light locked onto each other; dark, untidy shapes of mountains; glaring, angry eyes; raised and pointed knives; lunging, drunken figures … And these picturings are caused by the writer's words, although each reader will picture in his own way (that is where we are all modestly original); the words do not determine exactly, they *underdetermine* what we actually picture. This is so whether we regard the passage as fiction or fact. The passage could equally well be an extract from a diary or an extract from a novel, but the picturings it prompted could be the same in each case. The distinction between fact and fiction need not affect the trail of imaginings that accompanies our reading or listening like the phosphorescent wake of a ship at night, but it does, of course, have other effects. If we take the passage to be an extract from a diary, we believe the author to be asserting a string of propositions about the actual world; if we take it as fiction, we imagine (pretend to ourselves) that he is doing so, although we do not believe he is.

We see that there are three levels at which imagination operates when we apprehend literature. First, in the case of fiction, it operates in our overall make-believe that what we read or hear are genuine assertions, questions, complaints, commands, etc. This is our continuous and collusive engagement in the make-believe activity to which the author invites and seduces us. Second, the author's words, etc. cause us to picture what the words describe. Third, in the case of plays and films, the actors (props, camera crew, designers, etc.) cause us to seem to be watching real people, places, etc., not actors in greasepaint, painted flats, a succession of photographic images projected onto screens, or electronically transmitted patterns of dots and lines. While at the first level our imagining is normally voluntary, at the other levels it is normally involuntary. We may, indeed, with some effort, choose to see the person we observe before us as Gielgud, not Prospero, and, with more effort, see the patterns we perceive on the screen as just patterns, not dinosaurs; but we cannot choose, just then, when he is acting Prospero, to see Gielgud as Falstaff, or, just then, when we see dinosaur patterns on the screen, to see those very patterns as Mickey Mouse. The skill of the author, director, actors, designers, etc. consists in their ability to induce in us, usually with our collaboration, the illusion, which we know all along is an illusion, that things are going on which are not in fact going on. At this second and third level of imagining, notice that, as it has sometimes been put, the self is always present. When we imagine Anna Karenina stepping towards the train, we imagine *ourselves* watching her stepping towards the train. When, watching the actor Sir John Gielgud recite 'I'll break my staff … ' we imagine Prospero in *The Tempest* declaring he will break his staff,[10] we imagine *we* are watching Prospero making the declaration (and this is so

78

even, say, in dreams in which we seem to observe ourselves from without – it is *we* who seem to observe ourselves) .

Most philosophers have ignored this aspect of imagining. They do not recognise the part that illusion has to play in our apprehension of fictional works. Kendall Walton, for instance, claims only that fictional works are 'props' for our imaginings.[11] That is, the author of a novel writes sentences which prescribe what we are to imagine, the actors in a play 'mandate', together with the author, what the audience is to imagine. But they do not, he seems to think, *cause* our imaginings, nor does he appear to recognise that, when we apprehend a fictional work, we may undergo the self-aware *illusion* that we are watching Prospero or witnessing the last moments of Anna Karenina's life. On his view, it seems, our make-believe never involves illusion, even though it is illusion that we know is illusion.

This is an error of omission. That the author prescribes what we are to imagine is true, and we have incorporated this insight into the account of imagining we have just given. Certainly, people who imagine Anna Karenina as a citizen of Monaco have failed to make-believe as Tolstoy prescribed, have broken the rules of the game. They are as mistaken as is someone who, purporting to be playing chess, moves the castle diagonally across the board. But there is far more to an author's work than just laying down the rules of the game, and that is what Walton's account omits. When we watch *The Tempest*, we understand, of course, that we are to imagine that there is an old man, Prospero, his young daughter, Miranda, a monster called Caliban, and a spirit, Ariel. ... We understand that we are to imagine that at one point Miranda declares 'Oh brave new world, that has such people in it!' But there is much more to our make-believe than that. Shakespeare, the director, actors and stage designers, all collude with us to *cause it to seem* to us that what is actually a stage and some bits of machinery is an island, and that someone painted and dressed up and reciting words is Prospero or Ariel or Miranda. We undergo the illusion that these things are so – the author, director, stage-designers and actors produce, with our co-operation, the illusion that they are. We do see an actor as Prospero, we do see an actress as Miranda, and another actor as Caliban, just as we do see the straight stick half-immersed in water as bent. We know that this is an illusion.

What has led philosophers to neglect this may well be the mistaken thought that someone undergoing an illusion has the false belief that things really are as the illusion presents them. From this it is easy to conclude that the audience of a play or other fictional work cannot be undergoing an illusion (at least, so long as they retain their grasp of the fact that the work is fictional). For they do not falsely believe that they are witnessing the behaviour of real people called Prospero, Miranda, Ariel and Caliban. But the premise of that argument, as we have seen, is false. Many an illusion is an illusion that we know we have, and so it is in this case. We pretend to ourselves that the young girl reciting on the stage is Miranda on a magical island. Pretending to ourselves here may, and if successful, often does, consist in *seeming* to see a magical island, a magician, his daughter and a monster, although it does not, of course, also consist in *believing* that is what we really see. In their failure to recognise this, theorists diminish the author's role from that of cook to that of recipe-writer.

Conclusion

These remarks are a step towards a theory of the imagination, but they do not constitute that theory. Nevertheless, they do illuminate some features of the opaque concept of imagination in terms of the clearer notion of make-believe, or pretending to oneself, and of deceptive and nondeceptive illusion. A satisfying consequence of this, albeit partial, illumination is that we can now see how fiction, our psychological responses to fiction and often our mere apprehension of the spoken or written word all involve imagination. We have also already seen, in Chapter 3, that one of the keys to imagination (nondeceptive pretence) will unlock some of the mysteries of irony, too; in the next chapter we shall see that it will open metaphor's door as well. We can begin to discern, in other words, what may be the lineaments of a unified theory.

6

METAPHOR

Prologue

Some literature is highly figurative, and of all the figurative uses of language, metaphor (including synecdoche and metonymy) is perhaps the most pervasive and fundamental – so much so that some theorists have said all language is metaphorical, while some critics have regarded whole works as extended metaphors. Whether or not these claims are valid (the first, we shall see, could not be), we certainly ought to get clear about what metaphors are. Other types of figurative language are not as problematic, and so do not need, or attract, such close philosophical attention.[1]

A theory of metaphor should at least explain the difference between metaphors and their close kin, similes, what kind of linguistic act a metaphorical utterance is, and how it comes about that some metaphors, declining into dead metaphors, are eventually embalmed as additional senses of words. Many theories of metaphor have addressed these issues, but some have neglected or underestimated an essential point: metaphorical utterances are not illocutionary acts, any more than fictional or ironical utterances are; they are, like them, *para-illocutionary* acts. Just as the fiction-maker who says, 'Once upon a time there was a frog prince,' is not really asserting there was once a frog that was a prince, and the ironical hostess who says, 'I'm so glad you could get here early!' to a tardy guest is not really asserting that she is delighted at his early arrival, so the metaphorist who says, 'John was totally burned up,' is not really asserting that John was wholly incinerated. In all these cases the speaker is uttering a sentence that could be used to make an assertion in order to do something different and more sophisticated. In general a metaphorical utterance is one in which the utterer produces a form of words which could constitute or be part of an illocutionary act while actually using it to perform a different and more sophisticated linguistic act. It takes time to learn how to do this, and ingenuity to do it well, just as it does to learn to perform any para-illocutionary act. For para-illocutionary acts involve exploitation of previously mastered illocutionary ones; illocutionary acts stand to para-illocutionary acts as scales stand to sonatas: we progress from one to the other.

Some features of metaphors

Before we go any further, we ought to remind ourselves of the kind of things we are talking about, and note some of their features. Here are a few examples, drawn from literature or ordinary speech, some of them all too familiar to philosophers:

1   Sally is a block of ice.
2   What you said yesterday really burned me up.
3   Christ was a chronometer.
4   An intellectual is a man or woman of thoroughbred intelligence who rides his mind at a gallop across country in pursuit of an idea.
5   The barge she sat on, like a burnish'd throne
    burn'd in the water.
6   The trial, which took place over the following weeks, was like a circus, although there was some difficulty getting the elephants into the courtroom.
7   The gentle seaslides of saying I must undo.
8   Was it raining cats and dogs?
9   What a dream of a dress!
10 Life is not a bed of roses.
11 Bill is a limp lettuce.

This is a fairly limited range of examples, but even so, it supplies food for thought to browse on. There are several observations we can make right away. First, we can often see a close relation to similes. Someone who uttered the simile:

(1a) Sally is like a block of ice

might well be accomplishing the same sort of end as would be accomplished by uttering (1). This has perhaps led to the theory, to be discussed in the next section, that metaphors are no more than elliptical similes.

Second, while metaphors sometimes turn on a single word or expression, that is by no means always the case. For instance (5), from Shakespeare's *Antony and Cleopatra*, does turn on the use of 'burn'd' (if he had written 'shone' instead, there would have been no metaphor); yet (4), from Virginia Woolf, involves not just the single word 'thoroughbred', but also a number of associated terms drawn from the vocabulary of riding and hunting, which serve to extend and deepen the metaphor, and (6), from Woody Allen, turns not just on the use of 'elephant', but on the simile in which the metaphor is embedded, that the trial was 'like' a circus.

Third, all the metaphorical sentences above could be used to make literal statements or perform other literal speech acts. Someone could utter (5), for example, quite literally, to report the occurrence of a fire on the Nile, and (10) to utter a literal truth of numbing banality.

Fourth, in those two cases the metaphorical sentence could be used to make a true statement. But that is not possible for every metaphor, both because metaphorical sentences need not be cast in statement form (8) and (9), for example) and, more interestingly, because even when they are, many could be used only to make false or nonsensical statements. Thus, no literally true statement could be made by uttering Herman Melville's (3), Virginia Woolf's (4) or Dylan Thomas's (7), except (which is beside the point) by changing the reference or sense of some of the words (using 'Christ' as the name of a clock, for instance, or 'rides his mind' with the sense of 'thinks determinedly', or 'seaslides of saying' with the sense of 'continuously rhythmical speech'). As I am using 'sentence', that would make the sentence a different one. But, whether we use 'sentence' in that way, or in a way that allows the same sounds or marks with different senses and references to remain the same sentence, the distinction between such sentences and those that did not need any doctoring to become 'true statements' would remain: (10) could be used to make a true statement without such changes, whereas (3) could not.

Fifth, it follows from the fact that metaphorical sentences could be used to perform other speech acts that whether it is used to produce a metaphor is, as is whether it is ironic or fictional, a matter of the utterer's intentions. Either a madman or a poet may say 'Christ was a chronometer,' and the second may intend to speak metaphorically, the first to speak literally. Whether the sentence 'John's really on the mat now,' is a metaphorical reference to John's currently being reproved or a literal reference to his present whereabouts is a matter of the utterer's intentions. Sometimes both intentions may be present; if Red Riding Hood had shot the wolf before it reached her grandmother's house and sold its meat in the market, she might have been said both literally and metaphorically to have kept the wolf from the door. But while the utterer's intention determines whether an utterance is metaphorical, it may not always determine how the audience will treat it. A prattling child or a drunken roisterer may babble of blue fields in a swelling sea of shade, and neither need be uttering a metaphor; yet the audience may choose to treat what they say as one, just as some audiences may choose to take the bible as a work of allegorical fiction, not primitive historiography or divine revelation.

Sixth, metaphors are often applauded as 'true' or 'apt', sometimes condemned as 'false' or 'inept' or 'strained'. It would probably be less misleading to reserve 'true' and 'false' for the appraisal of literal utterances, and keep 'apt', 'inept' and the like for our criticism of metaphors; for to call a metaphor 'true' is to take a (possibly unconscious) step towards the theory that metaphors are all cast in the form of statements – which we have already seen is false – and that, in so far as they are, their main or even sole purpose is to do the same thing as statements (assert true propositions), only in a rival and roundabout manner – which we shall shortly see is false, too. Nevertheless, it must be acknowledged that our verdicts on many metaphorical utterances (e.g. 'Bill is a limp lettuce') are supported in the same way that our verdicts on statements are – by the production of evidence in the form of literal statements (e.g. 'It's true, he has no initiative or resolution'). This needs explanation.

Seventh, it is common to equate a vivid or striking metaphor with an apt one but, while they often coincide, they are not inseparable. An apt metaphor is not necessarily vivid or striking and a vivid one is not necessarily apt. 'Bill is a limp lettuce' (11) may be, or once have been, vivid, but if Bill is assertive and tough, it is certainly not apt. On the other hand, in (5), the metaphor that Cleopatra's barge 'burn'd' in the water may be considered apt, rather than striking.

Eighth, mention of fading metaphors should remind us of the fact that a metaphor, unlike a simile, can die, while (8) is so moribund, if not already dead, that we scarcely pay any more attention to it than we would to a sentence like 'Was it raining a lot?' (itself a dead metaphor). Most dead metaphors have been preserved as secondary senses of words. The mouth of a river is not a mouth in the original sense, nor is the eye of a needle an eye in the original sense, yet 'mouth' and 'eye' have come to have the dead metaphor as secondary senses. On the other hand, the metaphor of raining cats and dogs, which is as dead, or nearly so, as that of the mouth of a river or the eye of a needle, has not been preserved in this way – presumably because we do not have a word here like 'mouth' or 'eye', but a three-word phrase. When preservation does take place, though, there seems always to be an apparently significant resemblance we can point to: the mouth of a river and the eye of a needle resemble in a significant way those of an animal. The resemblance made the metaphor apt before it died, and afterwards eased its passing into a literal, if secondary, sense of the word. Notice that the resemblance need not be real; it need be only one that is believed to hold. Pigs may not be, and in fact probably are not, greedy, dirty, sulky, obstinate or annoying creatures, but the belief that they are so gave rise to the metaphorical use of 'pig', which has now died into a secondary sense of the word, so that to say that someone is a pig is to say that he has the, supposedly porcine, characteristics of being greedy, dirty, sulky, obstinate or annoying.

This is an appropriate point at which to turn to the relation of metaphors to similes, which are explicit statements of resemblance.

Metaphors and similes

We can often find a simile in some way associated with a metaphor, and this has led some thinkers from Aristotle onwards to argue either that metaphors have a metaphorical meaning that can be given by some literal simile, or that metaphors are really nothing more than elliptical similes. The idea here is that (1) for example either has the metaphorical meaning (1a) 'Sally is like a block of ice,' or is an ellipsis, or incomplete form, of that sentence. All we have to do, the theory in either variant goes, is to add 'like' or 'as' to the metaphorical sentence, and then we get either the metaphorical meaning of the original sentence or the sentence of which the original was an ellipsis.

At first glance these closely related views seem appealing, but when we consider them more carefully the attraction palls. In the first place, it is not always at all easy to find a suitable way of turning the original sentence into an appropriate simile. Adding 'like' or 'as' to (1) yields a perfectly meaningful sentence, whether or not it is the one the metaphorical one is alleged to mean or be an ellipsis of. But do we know where to add those words to (7), (8) or (9) so that the result is a literally meaningful sentence? 'Like the gentle seaslides of saying I must undo'? 'It was raining as cats and dogs'? 'What a like dream of a dress!'? These sentences are not even grammatical (although the last may, no doubt, occur in some dialects), so clearly we would have to do more than simply add 'like' or 'as' to obtain the literal version which is supposedly either the metaphorical meaning of the original sentence or its completed, nonelliptical form. In the second place, if a metaphor is an elliptical simile, since both are sentences, it must be an elliptical sentence; but an elliptical sentence is strictly one which needs some other words to turn it into a grammatically complete one. 'Sally is a ...of ice' is an elliptical sentence, then; but (1) is a perfectly grammatical sentence already. What is meant by calling it an elliptical one? Simply that it is synonymous with (1a)? But that is manifestly false. A translation of (1) into (1a) would be an incorrect translation, just as a translation of 'Janet is an Australian' into 'Janet is like an Australian' would be an incorrect one. But if it is now claimed that (1) is an ellipsis for (1a) because (1a) gives the metaphorical (not the literal) meaning of (1), the theory that metaphors are elliptical similes collapses into the theory that they have a simile as their metaphorical meaning. We shall see later that the idea that a metaphor has a metaphorical meaning, in the form of a proposition somehow conveyed by a sentence with a different meaning, is unsatisfactory. For the present we need only say that there seems no reason to prefer (1a) as the metaphorical meaning rather than some other sentence, such as 'Sally is emotionally unresponsive'. The theory that the *simile* is the metaphorical meaning is thus left unsupported even if, as I think we should not, we believe the metaphor does have a metaphorical meaning in the sense intended.

These difficulties render the suggestion that metaphors mean or are elliptical formulations of literal similes unattractive; but we should remember that the suggestion started from a truth: many metaphors can be explicated by means of a literal simile, and in many cases the job the one does could be equally well accomplished by the other. In the context of a discussion of Sally's emotional responsiveness, there is little, if anything, that (1) will bring to the audience's mind that (1a) will not. This truth, which the two related theories just discussed recognise but misinterpret, is one we must accommodate and explain in whatever theory of metaphor we eventually adopt.

The interaction theory

The theory, or rather theories, that go by this name start from the observation that in many metaphors there appears to be a relation between two semantic 'contents'. In 'Man is a wolf', for example, qualities associated with wolves are attributed to men. Put like that, the theory barely rises above a truism. Nevertheless, it looks less like a truism when we change the example and try to be a bit more precise. In (1), to put it one influential author's way,[2] there would be a 'principal subject', 'Sally', and a 'subsidiary subject', 'a block of ice', which have different semantic contents and the metaphor would involve an interaction between them. Still more precisely, a 'system of commonplaces' (not necessarily true commonplaces) usually applied to the subsidiary subject are applied to the principal subject. Thus lack of emotion would be attributed to Sally by means of 'implying statements' about Sally that normally apply to blocks of ice. When we ask what statements these are, the only one that seems at all plausible is that she is unemotional. We cannot say that she is cold, for instance, or hard. For she is only metaphorically either of these things, whereas blocks of ice are literally so; and it is literal statements about ice that, according to the theory, the metaphor applies to Sally.

This does not yield a 'system' of commonplaces, but just one statement, and one which albeit manifestly true, is scarcely a commonplace at all, in the way that 'Wolves are fierce and savage' is a commonplace about wolves. Who normally thinks of blocks of ice as lacking emotion in the way they think of wolves as fierce? Besides, as 'Sally', being a name, does not have a meaning in the ordinary sense of the word (for names do not in that sense have a meaning as 'block of ice' does), this account, taken strictly, is just wrong. We could easily amend it here, but it would still be unsatisfactory in other ways. For it is surely false that statements that normally apply to (i.e. are, or are commonly thought to be, true of) cats and dogs are implied about rain in the metaphor that it was raining cats and dogs. It baffles ingenuity to say what are the principal and subsidiary subjects in (7) 'The gentle seaslides of saying I must undo' ('gentle seaslides' and 'saying', or 'gentle seaslides of saying' and 'undo'?), while it does not so much baffle ingenuity as absolutely defy it to say how statements normally applying to the one – whichever it is

– are implied about the other. Moreover, the interaction view holds that there is a 'cognitive content' (in other words, a metaphorical meaning) which, even though it may not be paraphraseable, every metaphor conveys to its audience; and that, as we shall see in considering the next theory, seems to be false, too.

The trouble with this theory, as with so many, is that it is based on too limited a range of examples so that, when we widen the range, it falls patently short of the mark. This is not to deny, however, that very often a cognitive content can be supplied which at least matches the metaphor, or that in metaphors something we could call a principal subject and something else we could call a subsidiary subject can often be identified, and that attributes of the second are often implied to apply to the first, to which they do not in fact literally apply at all. What we are denying is that these are defining characteristics of metaphor.

Literal and utterer's meaning

John Searle has claimed that metaphors have a metaphorical meaning which can be explained in terms of the utterer's, as contrasted with the literal, meaning.[3] Clearly, this theory is kin to some of those we have already considered in that they all posit a meaning, in the form of some proposition, for a metaphor. The literal meaning, in the present theory, is just what the *sentence* means, whether it is uttered as a metaphor or not. The metaphorical meaning on the other hand is what the *utterer* of the sentence means. Thus, in (1), the literal meaning of the sentence is just that which the semantics and syntax of English determine – *Sally is a block of ice*. However, that is not what the utterer of the sentence means if he is uttering it as a metaphor. He means, at the least, that Sally is emotionally unresponsive. So part at least of the metaphorical meaning of (1) is that Sally is emotionally unresponsive. That, on this view, is the nucleus of the metaphorical meaning. However, there is an indefinite penumbra of associated thoughts that are also part of the metaphorical meaning – that Sally is grim, perhaps, or forbidding, indifferent to the feelings of others, humanly defective...

Why should people choose to use a sentence which means one thing to convey a different meaning altogether? If the utterer of the metaphor wants the audience to believe that Sally is emotionally unresponsive, why doesn't he just say so, instead of going about it in this roundabout manner? (This is a question for any theory that holds that metaphors are ways of asserting something other than what they seem literally to say, as we also saw it was for the traditional account of irony which claimed that irony consisted in saying one thing in order to convey the opposite.) How do they contrive to do it? To take the first question first: a possible answer is that both utterer and audience enjoy an indirect rather than a direct mode of communication. In other words, we like to play with language (which does not mean that we aren't being serious when we do so). Even if this answer is heading in the right direction, though, it has not reached its destination yet – we need to know what the attraction of this peculiar form of indirection is. The answer to the second question is that very general principles of interpretation require the audience to interpret the sentence so as to obtain an interesting, rather than a boring, reading of it. Confronted in the case of (1) with a sentence that, taken as a literal assertion, would be blatantly false, the audience casts about for what else the utterer might mean by it, and arrives at the conclusion that he means that Sally is emotionally unresponsive, and wishes to convey associated thoughts along with that one. Similarly, when confronted with (10), which, taken literally, would be boringly and obviously true, the audience casts about for what else the utterer might mean by it, and concludes that he means, at least, that life is not always pleasant. (This casting about is not supposed to be necessarily a conscious process which the audience is invariably aware of; it is a reconstruction of a process that must be presumed to have occurred, whether consciously or not.) This would not explain why the audience fixes on that interpretation, rather than on the apparently equally possible one that Sally is unintelligent – which is also a feature of blocks of ice – in the case of (1), or that success in life does not require a lot of patient work or occasional pain – which, in the case of (10), are both features of successful rose-cultivation. But the solution to that problem would be that the context in which the metaphor is uttered usually gives some clue to the audience as to which interpretation is intended; we do not receive metaphors in a vacuum but in a context, and against a background of shared knowledge and assumptions. Talk of Sally's being a block of ice arises in a context in which her emotional, not her intellectual, capacities are being considered, and talk of life's not being a bed of roses takes place in the context of a discussion about people's disappointment that things are not going as well as, rather than that they were going better than, they had hoped. This cues the audience, we might say, not to interpret the metaphor in (1) to mean that Sally is unintelligent, or that in (10) to mean that success in life does not require much patience and hard work.

On this view there is, in principle at least, a literal paraphrase of every metaphor which is what the utterer of the metaphor nuclearly means, the kernel of its metaphorical meaning. To utter a metaphor is, at least, to seek to convey that meaning to one's audience, just as to utter a statement is to seek to convey the proposition asserted to them. This is, I think, an advance on the other theories we have considered, while like them in holding that a proposition, stateable or not, is the metaphorical meaning of a metaphorical utterance. But, while it may contain some of the truth, it cannot be wholly correct. For an utterance need not, even in principle, be interpretable in the way suggested in order to be a metaphor. If it turned out that someone who said 'Virtue is profligacy cubed' had no further 'utterer's' meaning in mind, that he was unable to provide, even in principle, any literal paraphrase of his utterance, we would not be obliged to conclude he was not speaking metaphorically. It might perhaps be a poor, and would surely be an obscure, metaphor; but, if the utterer intended his utterance to be metaphorical, a metaphor it would be. It seems that this theory may have confused two separate questions here: what it is to be a metaphor and what it is to interpret one. Perhaps some metaphors are just not interpretable, in the sense proposed. That would not necessarily show even that they were bad metaphors, let alone that they were not metaphors at all.

Nevertheless, again, this theory is quite right to insist on the importance of literal paraphrases in our understanding of metaphor. We very often can and do give literal paraphrases in our explication of a metaphor, or respond to one by making a literal statement. 'What do you mean, Sally is a block of ice?' 'Well, she's emotionally unresponsive, isn't she?' 'Not at all. She has deep feelings, but she just doesn't show them easily'. – This is too typical a kind of conversation to be ignored; it must be acknowledged and explained in any satisfactory theory.

Denial of metaphorical meaning

An alternative approach holds that metaphors mean exactly and only what they say. On this view, put forward by Donald Davidson,[4] there need be no such thing as a further, metaphorical meaning, in the form of an in principle paraphraseable proposition, which is at least part of the utterer's meaning, nor any such thing as a literal simile which is the meaning of the metaphor or the completed form of an elliptical, metaphorical, sentence. The metaphorist, on the contrary, 'uses' the metaphorical sentence, with the one and, if unambiguous, only meaning it has, not to assert (if it is a declarative sentence) some definite proposition or cognitive content other than that which would have been asserted if the sentence had been uttered literally, but to 'evoke', 'intimate' or 'prompt' an indefinite range of thoughts, feelings, ideas, and images in the audience's minds – things which need not be and often are not propositional in character. On this view, 'Sally is a block of ice' means just that: Sally is a block of ice. Here the present theory and the previous one are in agreement. But, according to the present theory, the speaker uses the sentence, not to convey an 'utterer's meaning' in the form of some in principle paraphraseable literal proposition, but to 'intimate' or 'provoke' recognition of likenesses between Sally and blocks of ice. None of what is intimated needs be the proposition that Sally is emotionally unresponsive, which Searle's theory held was at least partly the metaphorical meaning – although that she was so would be one way of explaining some of what the metaphor evoked and was intended to evoke. If we were to use the words 'utterer's meaning', in connection with this theory, we should be speaking only of the utterer's *intention* to provoke recognition of likenesses between Sally and blocks of ice, not of some *proposition* he wished to convey as the metaphorical meaning of the sentence he uttered.

A main difference between the utterer's meaning account and this is that the first claims, while the second denies, that metaphorical sentences are intended to convey a proposition (the utterer's meaning, summarisable in principle in a literal paraphrase) different from that which the sentence itself expresses. As we have seen, the claim that this is what metaphors, essentially at least, are intended to do seems mistaken. So far the second theory seems to be correct. Another main difference is that this theory claims the distinctive character of a metaphor – what makes it a metaphor – is that it 'makes us see one thing as another by making some literal statement that inspires or prompts the insight'.[5] Thus, it appears, to utter the simile 'Sally is *like* a block of ice' is to attempt to get us to see *that* Sally resembles a block of ice (where 'seeing that' is believing), while to issue the metaphor 'Sally *is* a block of ice' is to attempt to get us to see her *as* a block of ice. We must construe 'see' here, presumably, not simply as 'visually perceive', but so as to include 'visualise' and 'think of' or 'imagine' (but not 'believe'). This, too seems plausible. When people say 'Hillary is a ball of fire', they provoke images associating Hillary with a glowing or burning globe – at least, if the metaphor has not yet gone stale. Allen Ginsberg's metaphor of 'angel-headed hipsters burning for the ancient heavenly connection to the starry dynamo in the machinery of night'[6] provokes vaguer, more varied and complex images associating hipsters with angels and the night with machinery housing a dynamo of or like stars.

Developing this thought a little further, we might say that trying to get us to see Sally as a block of ice is no doubt often a way of trying to get us to see that she is, like a block of ice, emotionally unresponsive; but that is one of the *effects* the metaphor accomplishes, not what it *is* or *means*. In these cases the metaphor accomplishes its effects by *prompting* us to notice similarities (or dissimilarities), not by codedly *stating* them. This, too, seems at least partly correct (although we shall see shortly it is not fully so). 'Joan's voice was a bell' prompts us to think of Joan's voice as (what it cannot be) a bell; 'Jack was a raging bull' prompts us to think of Jack similarly as a bull. 'Eleanor went through the roof' prompts us to think of Eleanor as (what she might conceivably have literally done) going through the roof. Thinking of them in these ways brings similarities to our attention. What we are thus led to conclude may well be propositional – Joan's voice was clear and pure, Jack was violently angry, Eleanor very so; but the thinking of or seeing *a* as *b*, which the metaphor *qua* metaphor provokes, is not propositional. Thus, it appears, a mistake of the other theories is that they confuse what we may seek to achieve by uttering metaphors – one of their purposes – with how we seek to achieve it – what they are.

Moreover, this account, or one like it, can provide answers to the three questions which we have so far left hanging in mid-air, tantalisingly unanswered. How are we to explain the fact that literal similes and corresponding metaphors seem sometimes to be virtually identical in their effect, if similes are essentially propositional in character whereas metaphors are not? Second, how do we apparently endorse or rebut metaphors by the production of literal statements (assertions of propositions) if the metaphor itself is not essentially propositional? Third, how do dead metaphors get embalmed as secondary senses of words if not by virtue of their having a propositional character which yields that sense? The answers to these questions turn out to be fairly straightforward.

First, similes and metaphors. The difference between them, if we regard only their effects, can indeed be, as one author has put it, negligible.[7] But this is not because they are essentially the same figure of speech. Rather, it is because, while being different figures, they sometimes seek to achieve the same object. 'Sally is a block of ice' prompts us to think of Sally as a block of ice, and thereby ultimately to consider whether there is some contextually relevant similarity between her and ice, namely, that both are emotionally unresponsive. The simile 'Sally is like a block of ice' does not prompt us to 'think of' Sally as a block of ice, but 'states' there is a similarity between her and blocks of ice, and thereby causes us to consider whether there is the same contextually relevant similarity between her and ice. (This is not to deny that we may also think of Sally as a block of ice when we hear the simile; it is to deny only that is what a simile necessarily sets out to do.) The end may be the same, but the means, which distinguish metaphor from simile, are different. Besides, as we have already seen, while appropriate literal similes can be associated with many metaphors, it is far from clear that they can be with all. In (1) the appropriate simile comes pat to mind. But what are we to do with Dylan Thomas's metaphor in (7) of undoing the gentle seaslides of saying, or with the same author's:

> The dens of shape
> Shape all her whelps with the long voice of water?[8]

These admittedly enigmatic utterances can still provoke images despite their opacity; but it is difficult to discern a precise literal simile which we should offer as appropriately associated with the metaphor.

Second, the use of literal statements to endorse or rebut metaphors. Given what we have just noticed, it is easy to see why literal statements are often made in response to metaphorical utterances. Where a purpose of a metaphor is to suggest that something is the case, the audience may well respond by giving evidence for or against the suggestion. Thus, confronted with Melville's (3) 'Christ was a chronometer', someone may reply 'But Christ wasn't at all a precise or matter-of-fact kind of person'. In doing so, they would not be reacting to some literal proposition which was the meaning of the metaphor; for there is no such proposition; they would be reacting to a proposition which the metaphor, by presenting Christ as a chronometer, had suggested to them. The very same suggestion could have been made by the simile 'Christ was like a chronometer', but neither that simile nor the proposition brought to mind by the metaphor would have been the meaning (even the metaphorical meaning) of the metaphorical sentence. In the same way, in response to the utterance 'I'm free on Thursday', someone may say 'Sorry, I've got an engagement'. That is a response to the proposition that they should meet on Thursday which is *suggested* by, but not the *meaning* of, 'I'm free on Thursday'.

Third, dead metaphors. It might seem that it was because metaphorical sentences like *The river's mouth is wide here* were used to convey the proposition *The river's outfall is wide here*, that 'mouth' came to have its secondary sense of 'river's outfall'. Hence it might be thought that metaphors must after all have some meaning, propositional in character, which allows the metaphor to decline, die and be embalmed as a secondary sense of a word. But, again, we can see how this misdescribes the facts. We can assume that when such sentences were living metaphors, they prompted their audience into, among other things, thinking of river outfalls as mouths. That was the metaphor. A purpose of such metaphorical utterances was to draw the audience's attention to the width of the river's outfall. Although the sentence did not at first mean 'The river's outfall is wide', familiarity with the image bred contempt, and the audience, ceasing to think of rivers' outfalls as mouths, began to go straight to the purpose of the metaphor (to draw attention to the width of the river's outfall) without travelling through the intervening medium of the metaphor. Hence, 'mouth' acquired a secondary sense of 'river's outfall'. This process does not entail, nor is it the case, that the metaphor had a propositional content which was its meaning all along; if it had, it would not have been a metaphor, but a code.

To these remarks we can add one more: an answer to the question why it is that we choose a roundabout way to bring about the belief that Sally is emotionally unresponsive. If that is what we utter the metaphor for, why not be direct and simply say that she is? I suggested that some might wish to answer that we like to play, and indirectness is a form of play here. We can now elaborate that thought a little. The metaphor is essentially an attempt to get us to see, or think of, Sally as a block of ice. It is not essentially a roundabout way of asserting that she is emotionally unresponsive. The metaphorist may wish to suggest that thought; but only as a consequence of seeing, or thinking of, Sally as a block of ice, thereby prompting the audience to notice significant resemblances between Sally and ice blocks. To say straight out that she was emotionally unresponsive would have been to omit the imaginative bridge between Sally and blocks of ice across which we travelled to reach that proposition. To the question 'Why travel across that bridge when you can reach the destination at once?' we can answer that the journey in itself gives pleasure. To travel pleasantly may be as good as to arrive.

Para-illocutionary acts

This account is in general satisfactory, then, but still it needs some amendment. First, we should notice that it is not only similarities that a metaphorist may wish to draw attention to, but also dissimilarities. When Donne uttered the metaphor 'No man is an island', he was drawing attention to *differences* between men and islands, not to resemblances. Second, we noted earlier that the theory held that it was by making 'a literal statement' that metaphorical utterances made us see one thing as another.[9] This is a mistake. The sentence that is uttered metaphorically is not – where it is one that could be so used – used to make a literal *statement* at all. Whatever else he may be doing, someone who metaphorically utters the sentence 'Life is not a bed of roses' is not making the tediously true literal statement that life is not a bed of roses, although that sentence could be used nonmetaphorically to utter that truism. If he were, his utterance would be assessable along two dimensions: literal truth and metaphorical aptness. But, except in those rare cases when the author wishes to speak both literally and metaphorically in the same breath, it is not. An interlocutor who seriously commented, 'Yes, that's quite true. Life is a quite different kind of thing from rose beds', would have missed the whole point of the utterance, not just the metaphorical point of it. No literal statement to that or any other effect was made.

The present theory misrepresents the character of metaphorical utterances in this respect. What makes them metaphors is not that they are illocutionary acts of stating, performed for the ulterior purpose of prompting recognition of similarities and dissimilarities; for they are not illocutionary acts at all. In so far as the utterances are purely metaphorical, they are what we have called (in Chapter 3) para-illocutionary acts: acts in which the utterer produces a sentence that could be used to perform an illocutionary act in order to perform an altogether different kind of act. What is this different kind of act? The act, I suggest, of nondeceptively pretending to perform an illocutionary act (stating, asking, commanding, promising or whatever) in which *a* is represented as (or as not) *b*, in order to draw attention to ways in which *a* is significantly like (or unlike) *b*. Someone who says metaphorically that Christ was a chronometer utters a sentence that could be used to make a statement. But stating is not his aim; on the contrary, he wants his audience to recognise that his apparent assertion is only apparent; in other words, that it is a mock- or pretend-assertion attributing chronometerhood to Christ. The purpose of the mock-assertion is to bring the audience to see contextually relevant similarities between Christ and chronometers. In this way, the metaphorist is like the ironist: each nondeceptively pretends to perform an illocutionary act in order to draw the audience's attention to something – the ironist to the gap between what would make the illocutionary act appropriate and how things actually are, the metaphorist to contextually relevant resemblances or differences between things, and that shows why the claim, mentioned at the beginning of this chapter, that all language is metaphorical is extravagant. Para-illocutionary acts are parasitic on illocutionary acts. In order to have the one, you must already have the other. So if there are metaphors, there must be literal utterances, just as, if there are parasites, there must be hosts.

We can describe and extend the conclusions we have reached in a more perspicuous way, using a little more of the vocabulary of speech act theory which we referred to in Chapter 2. Let us call the aim someone has in performing an illocutionary act – what he performs it *for* – a *perlocutionary* aim or intention, and the effect he thus brings about (if he succeeds) a perlocutionary effect. In a metaphor the utterer performs the para-illocutionary act of uttering a sentence that could be used to perform some illocutionary act without actually performing any illocutionary act. The act the utterer does perform is the para-illocutionary one of nondeceptively pretending to perform an illocutionary act in which *a* is represented as, or as not, *b* (Sally as a block of ice, Christ as a chronometer, saying as (composed of) seaslides, seaslides of saying as having to be undone, no man as an island...), with the perlocutionary aim of getting the audience to recognise similarities or dissimilarities between them. It may also be a further perlocutionary aim that the audience form certain beliefs on the basis of those similarities or dissimilarities. But that is still a perlocutionary aim, distinguishable from the para-illocutionary act of pretending to describe or represent *a* as, or as not, *b*. In the same way, a perlocutionary aim of saying that the water is boiling is typically to get the audience to *believe* the water is boiling, and a further perlocutionary aim may be to get them to *make the tea*; both of these are effects achieved by, but not identical with, the act of *asserting* that the water is boiling which was performed for those purposes.

Conclusion

I have not discussed the second claim mentioned at the beginning of this chapter, that a whole work of literature may be, or be seen as, one large, extended metaphor. But the discussion we have now completed shows that 'metaphor' is being used in that claim in a different sense from the one we have just investigated. It is hard to see how a literary work could be regarded as (literally) one large, or a series of, para-illocutionary acts of the metaphorical variety. When critics say that whole works are metaphors, they mean, apparently, that a leading metaphor keeps recurring in them, or that they are in some way symbolic or allegorical. No doubt they are usually right. However, the claim is not the exciting and controversial one it appears to be, that the works are literally metaphors, as 'Christ is a chronometer' is, but the far tamer one that they are symbolic or allegorical or have a metaphorical *Leitmotif*. Whether that claim is right or not is not a matter of what metaphors are, but of whether the proposed interpretation of the work is the right, or at least a reasonable, one.

So far as concerns the discussion of metaphor, that is not a question of any moment; but interpretation itself is. What makes a good interpretation? What is it legitimate to consider and what not? Some of these questions will be addressed in the next chapter.

7

INTERPRETATION AND INTENTION

Prologue

A literary author writes or speaks words; so does a historical, legal, philosophical, political, scientific, and every other kind of author. There may always be questions about what the words they uttered were, what they meant, what force they had, and what they entailed or implied. These are different questions, often indiscriminately lumped together under the all-purpose heading of 'meaning'. The task of the interpreter, whether literary critic, philosopher, scientist, lawyer or just everyday interlocutor, is to answer them. That is a task we all perform all the time. In the case of literature, the task is sometimes, though by no means always, harder to perform than it is in other domains.

What role does the author have in all this? In interpreting a work, are we – or should we be – trying to discover what the author 'meant' (in the various senses of 'meaning' mentioned above), or, rather, to find the best interpretation of the text he produced, regardless of whether it is also the interpretation the author intended? Some theorists have argued that, in literature at least, the author's intention is usually unavailable to the interpreter and in any case unnecessary for the interpretation of his work. To seek the author's intention, according to this view, is to commit the 'Intentional Fallacy'. In more recent times, Deconstructionists and other postmodernists have, rather more rhetorically, maintained a similar view: the author, they say, is 'absent' from his text, and therefore cannot communicate some intended meaning to his audience:[1] if anything, it is the reader who 'makes' the text. Others have argued on the contrary that the principal, or even sole, task of the interpreter is to discover what the author's intentions were. Debates between these different schools of thought have sometimes been conducted at a level of generality that has left the issues obscure. Perhaps attention to the various particular ways in which terms such as 'meaning', 'intention', 'text' or 'work' are used, and to the ways in which literary works differ from nonliterary ones, will help to clarify the matter. In what follows we shall be asking the same question about different aspects of a literary work, from the simplest to the most complex: how relevant is the author's intention to the interpretation of his work? As we shall see, we do not always get the same answer.[2]

Establishing the text

For any speech act, whether it is an ordinary conversation, a work of philosophy or an obscure poem, questions can arise about what the author actually said or wrote. Phone lines can be noisy, voices blurred, or ears inattentive, so that it is not clear to the audience what the speaker said. Did Tom say 'I met an earl last night,' or 'I met a girl last night'? Similarly, manuscripts can be damaged, writing indistinct, copiers sleepy, so that it is not certain what the author wrote. Did Shakespeare write (in *Hamlet*[3]) 'O that this too, too solid flesh should melt', or 'O that this too, too sullied flesh should melt'? How relevant would knowledge of the author's intention be, if only we had it, in answering this very simple kind of question? Certainly, it would not determine what he actually wrote or said, for there are slips of the tongue and pen, so that someone may fail to say or write the words he intended to. The celebratedly unfortunate Dr Spooner did not, presumably, intend to address his rural congregation as 'worthy tons of soil', yet those are, perhaps apocryphally, alleged to be the words he actually said. Shakespeare might have intended to write 'sullied', but actually have written 'solid' or *vice versa*.

But though the author's intention in this case does not determine what he actually wrote or said, it would normally be authoritative in establishing his (written or oral) text. That is, we would treat his intention at the time of writing, or publishing, if it was available, as providing the correct, or corrected, reading. If we knew that Shakespeare intended to write 'sullied' and that it was only a slip of the pen that prevented him from doing so, editors would be justified in correcting the text to accord with his intention, just as they would be justified in correcting a spelling or punctuation deviation where it was known that the author did not intend to depart from the accepted conventions. For in establishing the text we seek to establish, not simply what words he did utter, but also what words the author would have uttered if such accidents had not caused him to mispronounce, misspell or mispunctuate them; and that is a matter of his intentions. The infelicitous Dr Spooner did not insult his rural congregation by calling them tons of soil, although they might well have thought he did and been offended; he misspoke an inoffensive and apt description of them as sons of toil. A principle of both charity and clarity enjoins us to correct, or allow corrections of, such slips, for we thereby rescue the author's utterances from his misexecution of them.[4]

There may, indeed, be occasions when editors would wish to preserve the errant reading because it was in some way more interesting than the corrected one. If we knew that Shakespeare meant to write 'sullied', but by a slip of the pen wrote 'solid' instead, 'sullied' would be the word that should appear in his text. Yet we might well think in that case that he would have done better to write 'solid' which fits the idea of melting and the other ideas in the context better than 'sullied' does. In that case, the uncorrected reading might be given alongside the corrected one; but as a point of literary interest, not as a variant text of Shakespeare's play. In the same way, a printed edition of the mispronounced sermon would not read 'worthy tons of soil', even though those were the words the preacher actually said, any more than it would include occasional 'ums' and 'ers', although they, too, were what he actually said; but it might well point out, as a matter of personal and linguistic interest, that he did mistakenly utter those words.

At the basic level of slips of the tongue or pen, then, and of faulty spelling and punctuation, what the author meant to write or say (which is not necessarily what he *did* write or say, nor what he *says* he meant to) would, if only we could find it out, have authority. But can we find it out? Some may doubt it, thinking perhaps that an author's intentions are unrecoverable once his words have been written and he is 'absent' from his text. Such scepticism is unjustified. Even if we cannot know for sure, we can often make a good estimate of an author's intentions. They have, of course, to be inferred from what he says and does. But in this they are no different from other, nonlinguistic, intentions. All our beliefs about people's intentions (excepting, usually, our own) are formed on the basis of what we know and observe about them, but that does not prevent us from making justified estimates of what they intend.

To explicate this in rather obvious detail, if there were independent evidence that Shakespeare often misspelt 'solid' as 'sullied', for instance, or that Dr Spooner was indeed as inveterate a producer of Spoonerisms as he is made out to be, that would make it probable that Shakespeare intended to write 'solid' and that Dr Spooner intended to say 'sons of toil'. The probability would be increased by evidence in Shakespeare's case that 'solid' would fit the rest of the text better than 'sullied', that he did not have a chaotic mind and that he preferred harmony to disharmony in his literary style; if we had been able to interrogate him personally, the probability would have been still further increased by evidence that he said he meant 'solid', that he did not suffer from amnesia, and was not a liar. In the preacher's case, the probability would have been similarly increased by evidence that on the occasion of his sermon he was not out to offend his audience or parody himself, and that in the rest of the sermon his congregation were alluded to as deserving labourers, rather than heaps of dirt. Some of this evidence is available to us, some is not. On what we have, we can make a reasonable judgement. The fact that sometimes, or even most of the time, we cannot be certain beyond all doubt does not mean that we can form no idea at all of what each author meant to write or say. Where we do not have knowledge, we often have well-grounded belief.

Interpreting the text: the locutionary level

Once the text has been established, questions may arise at various higher levels about what it, in various senses, means. We may wonder, for instance, which sense an ambiguous word should bear in the context of a particular line, whether an allusion is being made, whether a passage should be read literally or rather as irony or metaphor, whether a character is being presented in one way or another, whether the moral of the story is this or that ... Adopting the terminology we used before (in Chapters 2 and 3), we can say that these questions arise at the locutionary level (which sense an ambiguous word should be given); the illocutionary level (whether some allusion is being made); at the parallel para-illocutionary level (is the passage metaphorical or ironical?), and, finally, at the as yet unnamed suprasentential level, at which we ask more general questions about what some part of the work, or the whole thing, means. (Is Shakespeare's Othello too generous a spirit to suspect Iago or just too much of a simpleton to see through him? Is his *Hamlet* about thought and action, revenge, madness, or the Oedipus complex – to name a few of the many proposals?) Let us ascend to these levels gingerly, one by one, beginning with the locutionary level.

In Donne's poem *A Valediction: Forbidding Mourning* occurs the following verse, which rival theorists have frequently crossed swords over:

> Moving of th' earth brings harmes and feares,
> Men reckon what it did and meant,
> But trepidation of the spheares,
> Though greater farre, is innocent.[5]

It appears that the phrase: 'moving of th' earth' could in Donne's time bear two senses, or meanings: the earth's upheaval during an earthquake, or its orbiting round the sun. Which sense should we assign to the phrase here? We know that Donne knew about and was interested in 'the new science', according to which the earth rotated round the sun, and so could have meant 'moving of the earth' in that sense. But in deciding which sense to give the phrase in the poem, should we seek to discover which sense Donne intended it to have, or should we rather consider which sense yields a more satisfactory reading of the poem, regardless of which sense Donne may have had in mind?

Taking one side in a debate that had been going on for years, Wimsatt and Beardsley, the authors of the influential paper 'The Intentional Fallacy',[6] argued that Donne's intention was as irrelevant as it was unavailable, and that we should consider only what made the best critical reading of

the poem. This did not mean that we should disregard all biographical information about the author, for that could be evidence of what the words he
wrote meant at the time he wrote them. But it did apparently mean that, if
we found Donne had intended the phrase in one sense, while the other sense
gave a better critical reading – however either of these conclusions might be
established – then we should interpret the phrase in the second sense. The
reasoning behind this view was that, first, the interpreter's aim should be to
find the best reading or readings of the poem, not what was going on in the
author's mind when he wrote it; second, what was going on in the author's
mind – what he intended – did not necessarily yield the best reading; third,
the materials for the best reading lay to hand in the text of the poem – the
meanings which the words of the text had at the time it was composed – and
allied information relevant to that text. Considering the text, Wimsatt and
Beardsley went on to argue that it plainly supported the reading of 'movements of th' earth' as earthquakes; for that made better sense of other
phrases in the verse and of other verses in the poem.

No doubt they were right as to which sense of 'moving of th' earth' gave
the better reading in the context of the poem in which the phrase occurred,
and assuming that Donne was selecting the words he used with some delib-
eration, it is surely likely that reading was also the one he intended. But
Wimsatt and Beardsley's point is that the question whether it was or was not
what he intended is a question about what the *poet meant*, not what the
poem means. What the poem means is established by the text the poet
produced, not by what the poet meant when he did so. 'There is a danger of
confusing personal and poetic studies', they wrote; 'and there is the fault of
writing the personal as if it were poetic'.[7]

On the other hand, some critics, such as E. D. Hirsch,[8] have maintained
that what a text means, hence, in this instance, whether it is earth's quaking
or orbiting that is meant by 'moving of th' earth', is a matter of what the
author intended. If Donne intended the phrase in the orbiting sense, regardless of whether that yields a more satisfactory poem (and regardless of how
we might discover his intention – clearly a matter of inference from whatever
evidence we can find), that is what the phrase means in that verse, and that is
how the verse should be interpreted. It is, we might say, the speech act
Donne performed in composing it. (In fact, upholders of the two views
would often engage in exactly the same critical practice; they would both
appeal to the evidence of the text for what was the right reading, for
instance. But the 'intentionalists' would claim they were thereby discovering
the author's intention as manifested in the text, while their opponents would
claim they were discovering only the most appropriate reading, regardless
whether it was also what the author intended.)

Which view is right? Given the hypothesis that we knew which sense
Donne intended for 'moving of th' earth' and agreed that the other sense
made for a better poem, which sense should we say was the correct reading?

The difficulty about answering this question is that it presupposes one of the two readings is *the* correct one, and that is a presupposition we should query. Certainly, if we want to know what *speech act* Donne performed in writing *A Valediction*, we need to know which sense of 'moving of th' earth' he meant. His intention would clarify what he was saying, what his speech act *was*. His verse is no different, in this respect, from a remark like 'The earth's moving makes people afraid', which he might have made in ordinary conversation to some contemporary. In order to know *what* remark exactly Donne was making, the contemporary would have had to know whether he meant 'moving' in the quaking or the orbiting sense, and it might have been that if Donne had meant the orbiting sense, he would have been wrong, whereas if he had meant the quaking sense he would have been right – perhaps people were not alarmed by terrestial orbiting, but were, naturally enough, by earthquakes. So here, in this quatrain, it might be that Donne intended the orbiting sense (although the evidence seems to go quite strongly against that), while in the context of the poem the quaking sense would have given a more satisfying reading. So far as correctly under-standing his speech act goes, Donne's intention, if we knew it, would be decisive.

But how far does that go? Why bother, an anti-intentionalist (whether of the Deconstructionist or the more traditional school) might ask; why bother with the 'speech act' interpretation, when a better is there to hand in the meanings which the words the poet used *could* bear? This is a legitimate challenge. It also helps to clarify the real issue between the intentionalists and the anti-intentionalists. We started by asking how far the author's inten-tions were relevant in interpreting his words. We have seen that, if we want to understand the poem as his speech act, his intentions, at least as so far considered, are authoritative. But the deeper question is whether we should restrict ourselves to understanding his speech act. Here we should notice a difference between ordinary conversation and poetry, or between nonliterary and literary discourse as a whole. In ordinary conversation, the audience's aim is usually only to discover what statement the speaker was making, or more generally, what speech act he was performing. Donne's interlocutor, in such a conversation, would have wanted to know whether he was asserting that it was the earth's quaking or the earth's orbiting which made people afraid. Once that was established, he would not normally have had any further interest, for current purposes, in the other proposition (whichever one it was) that the sentence Donne uttered could have been, but was not, used to assert. He would merely have wanted to get on with the business of considering whether what Donne actually asserted was true or not. But in the case of poetry, and literature generally, the audience's interests are not so practical and circumscribed. The quatrain from *A Valediction*, for instance, is offered, not (or not solely) as a statement to be assessed for truth or falsity, but also as a poem, a work of literature, to be appreciated for other

101

qualities than being true. If the poem would work better as a poem with the sense of 'moving' that Donne did not intend, we may well ask whether that is not the correct reading to give it.[9]

Thus, 'Which is the correct reading of the line?' would then be a question to which we would have to respond: 'Correct for which purpose?' For the purpose of determining what speech act Donne was performing (in other words, how he meant to be understood) the sense of 'moving' which he intended would clearly yield the correct reading. But for the purpose of obtaining the best reading of the poem, the sense he did not intend would be the correct one. This does not mean, of course, that in general an author's intentions at this level are irrelevant to the question which is the best reading of the poem, as some anti-intentionalists might hold; for the sense in which he intended his words to be understood normally would be the best reading of it, and would certainly be one which, if available, we would be wise to consider.

We have two possible interpretations of the poem at this level, the poet's and the most appropriate one. Normally, these two will coincide, but sometimes they will not. The anti-intentionalists are right in saying that what the poet intended is not necessarily the most appropriate reading, wrong in suggesting that what the poet intended is irrelevant. The intentionalists are right in saying that what the poet intended is relevant, wrong in claiming that it yields the reading we ourselves should give the poem. Both are wrong in suggesting that there is a correct reading independent of the purpose for which we are reading.

Interpretations and revisions

An objection might be lodged at this point. It is this: if the most appropriate reading of a poem is not the one intended by the author, yet is nevertheless a legitimate interpretation of what he wrote, why is it not also legitimate, when a slip of the pen yields the most appropriate reading (say, 'solid' for 'sullied'), to leave the error uncorrected? Is it not inconsistent to disregard the author's intention in one case, but not in the other?

No, it is not inconsistent; the two cases are different. When we correct slips of the pen and misspellings, etc., we are *establishing* the author's text, not interpreting it. We are not interested in what senses the words he used might bear, but in what words he either did utter or, save for executive mishap, would have uttered. Clearly, at that level, to print a different word is to distort his text, not to establish it. We can, of course, as we noted earlier, print the uncorrected slip as a point of literary interest. But we cannot print it as a legitimate variant of his text. On the other hand, once we have the text, we can legitimately interpret a word in a sense the author did not intend, provided it is a sense the word could bear in the linguistic community which constituted the work's primary audience. For then we are interested in getting the most appropriate reading of what he wrote; and that, while it may not be the reading he intended, is still a reading of what he wrote (or would have written but for executive slips in writing it).

If the author's intention as to which *word* he intended to write or say is available (by whatever means), it tells us which word we should print as his text; and if his intention is available as to which *sense* he was using an ambiguous word in, that tells us what his speech act was, what he intended us to understand; but it does not tell us what would be the best reading of the word in its context. Since, in reading a work of literature, we may want either to know what the author's interpretation of the word is, or what the best interpretation of the word, supported by the text, is, we may disregard the author's intention if our interest is the second one and his intention does not yield the best reading. We could, of course, go further than this if we wished. We could start changing some of the author's words or printing felicitous slips of the pen in his text, instead of correcting them. However, that would not be interpreting his work, but revising it.

In this respect literature is like music. A performer is not at liberty to change the notes that appear in a composer's score, unless he is justified in thinking the composer would have written other notes but for a slip of the pen. That is to say, he is not justified so long as he claims to be playing the composer's music. But he is entitled to play a passage with a different phrasing from the one we know the composer would have given it (but did not give in the score), if that makes the passage go better. In the first case, he would be changing the music the composer wrote; in the second, interpreting it differently from how the composer would have interpreted it. There is of course nothing wrong in itself with changing the notes or the phrasing in the score – but that, while it might make for better music, would not be a legitimate variant of the score or a legitimate interpretation of the work.

To illustrate this point more starkly: suppose that King James I had decreed that, from 1616 (the year of Shakespeare's death) certain words were to bear different and opposed meanings from those they previously had; suppose that his decree was obeyed and that he was clever or lucky enough to hit on meanings that yielded grammatical sentences when they were substituted for the meanings the words had before that date. Thus, the words 'O that this too, too solid flesh would melt' (assuming 'solid' was what Shakespeare wrote), when given their new meanings, might have meant 'O that this too, too melted flesh would jell.' It is conceivable (though vastly improbable) that these changes in meaning would have resulted, not only in grammatical sentences, but also in sentences that both made sense in themselves and, when connected, formed a coherent play. It would be as preposterous, however, to praise or censure Shakespeare for having written the play which thus ensued as it would be to praise or censure a vintner for the wine in his bottles that someone had adulterated with their own. For it would not be Shakespeare's play that we were reading, but a King James version based on Shakespeare's, just as it would not be the vintner's wine we were drinking, but an adulteration of the vintner's wine. However, if King James had discovered in 1616 that many ambiguous words used by Shakespeare were intended in one sense by the bard, but gave better readings when understood in their other sense, it would not be preposterous to read them in their unintended, but better, sense since we would not be changing what Shakespeare wrote, but choosing a better interpretation of it than his own.

Interpreting the text: the illocutionary level

Will this answer to the question of authorial intention hold when we ascend to the next level of 'meaning'? There seems to be no reason why not. Take an example from Wimsatt and Beardsley's essay. In *Love Song of J. Alfred Prufrock*, T. S. Eliot wrote:

I have heard the mermaids singing, each to each.[10]

This will call to some readers' minds a line of Donne's:

Teach me to heare Mermaides singing

(from the song 'Goe and catch a falling Starre').[11] Was the line that Eliot wrote an allusion to Donne's? Wimsatt and Beardsley claim that even an appeal to Eliot himself, who was still alive at the time, would not settle the matter. It might certainly tell us what was in the poet's mind, but that, they maintain, would have nothing to do with the poem. The 'way of poetic analysis and exegesis'[12] asks only whether it would make any sense to treat Eliot's line as an allusion to Donne's, and if Eliot said (truly) that he was alluding to Donne, while an allusion to Donne would not make any sense in the context of the poem, then Eliot's line did not allude to Donne's.

From the point of view of identifying Eliot's speech act, this is surely wrong. If Eliot had said truly that he wrote the line as an allusion to Donne, then the line would allude to Donne, just as if, in ordinary conversation, he had said truly that in remarking that he was going to catch a falling star, he was alluding to Donne's line 'Goe and catch a falling Starre', then he was alluding in that conversation to Donne's line. However, that is to view the matter from the point of view of the author's speech act, and we are not restricted to that point of view. It might well be that we would find the poem a better one if we did not think any allusion was made. Since we are not obliged to abide by the author's own interpretation, we should say that the correct interpretation of Eliot's line from the point of view of what his speech act was would be that it alluded to Donne's, while a better poetic interpretation of it from the point of view of the words he actually uttered would be that it did not. In so far as a reader aware of Eliot's intention was able to, he would be justified in disregarding Eliot's reading for the more appealing one which was not Eliot's, and his reading of the line would be a legitimate interpretation, not a revision, of it.

The same would be true, needless to say, about a passage that the author meant literally, but which would go better as irony or metaphor. To take a well-worn example: if his own testimony is to be believed, Housman was not being ironic when he wrote:

Oh God will save her, fear you not.
Be you the men you've been;
Get you the sons your fathers got
And God will save the Queen.[13]

Yet it might be thought that the poem works better if we take the lines as ironical (as indeed another author and critic, Frank Harris, assumed the author also intended them to be taken, only to be indignantly told by Housman that he did not).[14] The correct interpretation of them from the point of view of what Housman's speech act was would then be a literal one, whereas a better reading might be an ironical one. The reader could not be faulted for reading it ironically, provided he did not claim it was how Housman himself interpreted his words, what his speech act was.

It is worth noticing that what would be regarded as a better reading might vary with time. To jingoists at the beginning of the twentieth century the literal reading might seem better; to those living at the end of that century, after two world wars and countless others, the ironical one would more likely seem preferable. Similarly for metaphor: it is almost certain that when Donne wrote in the seventeenth century of our blood labouring 'to beget spirits, as like souls as it can,' he was using 'spirits' literally as 'the thin and active part of the blood ... a kind of middle nature between soul and body.'[15] Suppose we knew that. Still, it might be that a metaphorical reading of 'spirits' was also possible in Donne's time. It might well seem to a modern reader, if not to a contemporary of Donne's, that the metaphorical interpretation was better, although Donne intended the literal one. Then it would be a legitimate interpretation to take the word metaphorically.

Interpreting the text: the suprasentential level

What do we find when we go to a still higher level of 'meaning', to the level beyond that of the word or sentence? Now we come to general interpretations of whole works or parts of them. Is *Hamlet* about madness, revenge or the Oedipus complex? Was Anna, in *Anna Karenina*, a victim of society's conventions or of her own weakness? Was Iago, in *Othello*, gratuitously evil or motivated solely by jealousy of Othello? Questions like these can be asked about any work of literature and, while the answers are sometimes obscure and contestable, the method of answering them is the same. On the one hand, there is the author's interpretation, on the other there may be other interpretations of what he wrote; for the text may, and normally does, underdetermine what the answers to such questions are – that is, it may allow for various interpretations, rather than requiring one. The correct interpretation of his *speech acts* will be the one the author intended – so long, of course, as it is within the bounds of possible meanings of the words. (To take an extreme example, if Shakespeare had intended Othello to be a comic figure, then his words would have failed to realise his intention – he would have made Othello a tragic figure despite himself.) But we are not bound to accept the author's interpretation if a better one is licensed by the text.

We should notice here that the higher the level of 'meaning' is, the more underdetermined the text will normally be, and consequently the greater the licence will be for its interpretation. In many texts the context virtually rules out one sense of an ambiguous word (as it probably does in the case of Donne's 'moving of th' earth'). But when we come to such general questions as whether the theme of *Hamlet* is thought and action or madness, the text is less likely to exclude certain interpretations.

This underdetermination is sometimes due to the fact that when we ask questions at this level, we enter territory that the author himself is less likely to have explored. An author rarely uses an ambiguous word such as 'moving' in Donne's *A Valediction* without considering which sense he means (and he may, of course, mean both) and making that clear in his text. But Shakespeare might quite well have written *Hamlet* without once considering the question whether it was about thought and action or about madness; and if he had considered that question, he might well not have made up his mind. Hence, there is sometimes no authorial intention to discover, quite apart from the difficulty of doing so if there were. This underdetermination does not mean, however, that absolutely anything goes. Whatever interpretation is given must be licensed by the meanings of the words actually appearing in the text at the time they actually appeared. But it does mean that there is more room for an author's intention not to be realised in his words. To take another extreme case: Shakespeare might have intended Hamlet to be as much a man of action as Othello was, and believed that was how he had drawn his character, while the character emerging from the words he actually wrote was best construed as a paradigm of indecisiveness. Such mismatch of intentions with reality is unlikely enough at any time, but still less likely at the lower levels of 'meaning' we have been considering. If Donne meant 'moving of th' earth' in the quaking rather than the orbital sense, it is less probable that he wrote a line which did not make his meaning clear.

Conclusion

The relevance of the author's intention to the interpretation of his work is (apart from the matter of establishing just what exactly his text is) a matter of the purpose with which we read it. Every work can be approached from the point of view either of the author's own interpretation or of the best one. While knowledge of his intentions would settle many questions from the first point of view, it might not settle any from the second. Such knowledge will not of itself determine how his work should be interpreted, although it will certainly be relevant, and in interpreting the work, even if in fact what the author meant coincides with the best interpretation, we are not merely trying to discover what it was the author meant.

So far as fiction goes, much of what we have been discussing could have been put under the heading 'truth in fiction'. We could have asked: 'Is it true in the fiction *Hamlet* that the hero said 'sullied flesh' or 'solid flesh'? Or: 'Is it true in the fiction *Othello* that Iago was motivated by jealousy alone or also by a general desire to do evil rather than good?' Or: 'Is it true in the fiction *Anna Karenina* that Anna was a victim of her own frailty, or rather of society's rigid conventions?' But the question of truth in fiction, being wider than that, deserves a separate treatment; which it will get in the next chapter.

8

LITERATURE, TRUTH AND
MORALITY

Prologue

Two questions can arise about literature and truth. The first, as we briefly noticed at the end of the last chapter, concerns fiction alone: What is true in a work of fiction (or what is fictionally true in it), and how do we know it is? We can call this the question of truth in fiction. Some issues about what is true in fiction have no direct connection with the interpretation or appreciation of literature, and so are rarely discussed, or even noticed, by critics; but solving the issues does illuminate the concept of fiction itself, the nature of fictional worlds. The second question is one which critics and aestheticians have often discussed: What relevance does the truth or falsity of propositions which literary works convey about the actual (not the fictional) world have for their value as literature? We can call this the truth-relevance question. The first of these questions can be answered, the second clarified, with the help of the notion of implication. The truth-relevance question leads on to the morality-relevance question, that of the relation of the moral aspects of a literary work to its value as literature. Once misconceptions surrounding this third question are dispelled, the answer to it is fairly plain.

Truth in fiction

There was no such person as Anna Karenina in the actual world (let us assume so, anyway), but there is one in the world of Tolstoy's novel *Anna Karenina*. It is thus 'fictionally' true that there was a person called Anna Karenina. Another way of putting that is to say that it is true 'in the fiction' that there was a person called Anna Karenina. There are indefinitely many such fictional truths. It is also fictionally true (true in the fiction) that Anna was married, for instance, that she met Vronsky, that she left her husband, that she threw herself under a train. ... Anyone who knows the story can recite a multitude of such truths. It is, of course, what the author wrote that makes these statements true. If Tolstoy had not written the following sentence, or one relevantly similar to it, it would not have been true in his novel that Anna threw away her red bag before she threw herself under a train:

> But she did not take her eyes off the wheels of the approaching second truck, and at the very moment when the midway point between the wheels drew level, she threw away her red bag, and drawing her head down between her shoulders threw herself forward on her hands under the truck, and with a light movement, as if preparing to rise again, dropped on her knees.[1]

There are truths which are made so by the author's explicitly saying so. If Anna had been a real person, Tolstoy's writing that sentence about her would not have made it true that that real person threw herself under a train; it would have been an independent reality, what she did, that made it true. But in the fictional world of the novel, there is no independent reality. What the author says, goes (fictionally) – or usually so. If Tolstoy had written in his next sentence 'Anna did not throw away her bag, did not draw her head down, did not throw herself forward...' the reader would have been in a quandary. What actually would have happened in the novel? What would have been fictionally true in it? We could not hold that in the novel it is both true that Anna threw herself under a train and true that Anna did not throw herself under a train, although we can say that the author wrote each of these things. For two contradictory statements cannot both be true, whether in fiction or otherwise. In this case, what the author says does not go. Failing other evidence (e.g. of a slip of the pen, or that one of the sentences was a mistake), we would have to say that it was undeterminable whether in the story Anna threw herself under a train or not.

There seem to be other truths, however, which are made so, not by the author's explicit utterances, but by what his utterances logically imply. Tolstoy never wrote any sentence in *Anna Karenina* such as 'Anna had a vocabulary in Russian larger than two thousand words,' but by examining the sentences attributed to her in the book, we can deduce as a matter of logic that the proposition which that sentence expresses is true in the novel. For the utterances and thoughts attributed to her contain more than two thousand different words. Thus we see that the world of the novel extends beyond just what the author wrote. There are truths about it which are logically implied by, rather than explicit in, what he wrote.

There are still other truths which Tolstoy implies, although he does not imply them as a matter of logic. From the passage quoted above, we know that it is true in the novel that Anna threw away her red bag, but Tolstoy wrote nothing about whether it floated off into the air or landed a few feet away. Yet we are surely justified in believing that it did not float off into the air, that it must have landed a few feet away. Again he never wrote some such sentence as 'Anna had a heart and lungs,' nor did anything that he did write *logically* imply her possession of those organs. Nevertheless, we are equally surely justified in thinking she did have them – that is, in thinking that in the fiction it is true that Anna had a heart and lungs.

Why are we justified? Because of what is sometimes called 'conversational implicature' or, as I shall say, 'pragmatic' (as opposed to 'logical') implication.[2] There is a principle of ordinary communication that is not waived in such fictional cases as these, the principle that an audience should not be misled. Thus, suppose I am asked where the whisky is, and, knowing full well it is on the sideboard, I reply that it is either on the sideboard or on the table. That would normally be to mislead my audience into thinking I do not know exactly where it is. What I say is true, for if the whisky is on the sideboard, it must be true that it is either on the sideboard or on the table. Someone ignorant of its location who said it was either on the sideboard or on the table would have spoken truly, and the proposition they asserted would be the very one that I, knowing where the whisky was, also asserted. We would both have made true assertions, but their utterance would not have been misleading, while mine would have been. Theirs would have implied truly, whereas mine would have implied falsely, that the speaker did not know in which of the two places the whisky was. Thus my utterance would have contravened the principle that an audience should not be misled.

Now Tolstoy's descriptions of Anna in the novel all seem to imply that she is a normal human being with normal human organs. If she were not, he should have said so, for failing to say so would have been to mislead his audience. In nonfictional cases, that someone implies something is true does not, indeed, entail that it is so, as the example I gave just now shows – I may imply that I do not know exactly where the whisky is when in fact I do. This gap between what I imply and what is in fact true opens up because there is a fact of the matter – my knowing where the whisky actually is – which is independent of my implying either that I do or that I do not know where it is. In the case of fiction, that does not seem to be the case, for there is no independent fact of the matter apart from what the author says or implies. So just as, if Tolstoy writes 'Everything was upset in the Oblonskys' house', then it is true in *Anna Karenina* that everything was upset in the Oblonskys' house, so, if what he writes implies that Anna had a heart and lungs, then it is true in the novel that she had a heart and lungs.

Implication and the constitution of fictional worlds

The world of the novel thus seems to extend wider still. How far does it go? How many friends and acquaintances did Anna have, for instance? (Surely she would have known some people not mentioned in the novel?) How many teeth? (Surely there must have been a definite number at any given time?) Did she have whooping cough as a child? Did she have a tiny birthmark on the instep of her left foot? Did she live (when in Moscow) nearer to Omsk than to Khabarovsk? (Surely, in each of these cases, either she did or she didn't?) A critic might well be impatient of these questions, for they will usually have nothing to do with the literary merit of the book, and so will normally be irrelevant to critical concerns. 'Who cares?' might well be his response. Nevertheless, pursuing the questions will give us a fuller understanding of the nature of fictional worlds, an understanding that is worth having for its own sake, even if it has no bearing on our appreciation of fictions as literature. So let us persevere.

An intuitive answer to the questions posed above might go like this: We do not know, and cannot discover, exactly how many friends Anna had, how many teeth she had at a given time, whether she had whooping cough as a child, or whether she had a tiny birthmark on her left instep. But we can assume that she had a normal number of friends for her class and society, was not notably lacking in teeth, that, if she had whooping cough as a child, her health was not noticeably damaged by it, and that if she had a birthmark on her left instep, it played no significant part in her life, or that portion of it with which the novel is concerned. On the other hand, we can find out whether she lived nearer to Omsk than to Khabarovsk – all we need do is consult a map of Russia for the period of the nineteenth century in which the novel was set. If Moscow was nearer to Omsk than to Khabarovsk at that time, even if Tolstoy did not mention it, we know it is true in the novel that Anna lived nearer to Omsk than to Khabarovsk.

How might we try to justify this intuitive answer? Invoking the principle of pragmatic implication we have already cited, we might try this: Tolstoy's silence on the number of Anna's friends, on the number of teeth in her head, on whether she had whooping cough or a tiny birthmark makes it impossible to answer some of these questions exactly; but also, more importantly, it implies that she was in those matters normal for a woman of the class and time in which she is represented as living. That is why we can say that she probably had more friends than were mentioned in the book, was not toothless, and probably had some childhood diseases, although we cannot say what they were. Tolstoy's setting the story without qualification in nineteenth century Russia, however, implies that the geographical facts of that time hold in the story, too. So it is true in the novel that Anna lived, when in Moscow, nearer to Omsk than to Kharbarovsk.

How good, now, is this justification? It has a problem: what exactly did Tolstoy pragmatically imply by writing his novel as he did? The justification for the intuitive answer given above assumes that he implied that whatever was true of the actual (real) world was true in the novel, except where the story itself indicates otherwise. Thus, on this assumption, it is not true of the actual (real) world that there was in nineteenth-century Russia a woman called Anna Karenina who left her husband for a man called Vronsky and eventually threw herself under a train; but it is true in the novel that there was such a woman. On the other hand, it is true both of the actual world and in the novel that in the nineteenth century Omsk was nearer to Moscow than was Kharbarovsk.

But if this account of the matter is right, it will open the gates to a flood of fictional truths. For it is true of the actual world that the planet Pluto (which was not discovered till the twentieth century) existed in the nineteenth century, although no one then alive knew it did and, following the assumption, we would then have to say that it was true in the novel, set in nineteenth-century Russia, that the planet Pluto existed undiscovered. And not only the planet Pluto. There is a host of propositions true of the actual world that were not known in the nineteenth century at the time in which the story was set, nor, for that matter, at the time it was composed. To name only a few: that atomic energy was going to be discovered, men would walk on the moon, there would be a revolution in 1917, the Chernobyl nuclear power plant would have a serious accident towards the end of the century, and (going in the other temporal direction, towards the past) that men had travelled across the Baring Straits to modern Alaska in very early times. If Tolstoy implied that everything true of the actual world (and compatible with the story) was also true in the story, then he implied that a host of propositions that he did not know about were true; and, assuming (as consistency requires we should) that Homer (or whoever composed *The Iliad*) implied the corresponding proposition by setting his story in the Greece of his time, we would have to say that Homer implied exactly the same things were true in *The Iliad*, in so far as they were compatible with what was set down in the verses he composed.

Questioning the implications

This conclusion may seem too extravagant. What, we may wonder, has the existence of the planet Pluto got to do with the fictional world of *Anna Karenina*, let alone *The Iliad*? But, if we want to avoid the conclusion, we will have to change our assumption. We have been assuming that an author implies that everything true of the actual world is true of the fictional world, too, except where the fictional world is incompatible with the actual world. But perhaps that was wrong. Perhaps we should say, rather, that he implies only that whatever was generally 'believed true of the actual world in the society in which the fiction was composed' (and was compatible with the fictional world created in the fiction) is also true in the fiction. That would allow us to filter out a number of the propositions which our first assumption allowed in as truths. Since it was not generally believed in Tolstoy's time and society that Pluto existed, we could say it was not true in the novel that Pluto existed undiscovered. Also for Homer: since in Homer's society it was believed neither that Pluto existed nor that the world was round, it is not true in *The Iliad* that Pluto existed undiscovered or even that, although nobody knew it, the world was round. The fictional world, in other words, would be the actual world, not as it is, but as it was conceived in the society in which the fiction originated.

There are two other possibilities we could consider here. The first is that, instead of saying that what an author implies is related to what was generally believed to be true in his or her society, we should say that it was related to the time and society in which his/her fiction was set (as we suggested when we considered earlier whether Anna lived nearer to Omsk than to Khabarovsk). Then we would say that what was true in the fiction was what was *generally believed in the society in which the fiction was set* (and, of course, was compatible with the fiction itself). In the case of *Anna Karenina*, that would presumably make little or no difference, since Tolstoy set his novel in approximately his own society and times; but in other cases, it would make a substantial difference. In a novel such as William Golding's *The Inheritors*,[3] for instance, which was set in prehistoric times, it would be true neither that the world was round nor that there would be a revolution in Russia in 1917, although both these truths were generally believed in the mid-twentieth-century society in which the novel was composed and published. This approach filters still more out of the fictional world than the previous one, and keeps the fictional world more insulated from the real.

The second possibility would be to say that the author implies that it is what *his primary audience (or intended audience) generally believes* that is true in the fiction. Thus, an author might write for a special audience of flat-earthers, in which case it would be true in the fiction that the earth was flat, even though he never explicitly indicated that in his story. Or he might write for some anticipated posterity, intending his fiction to be published a hundred years after his death; and if his intended audience was going to believe that there was life on Mars, it would be true in his fiction that there was life on Mars, even though he did not make that explicit in his fiction, and whether or not it was true of the actual world.

Which of these approaches should we choose? Which assumption is most plausible? There will very rarely be a reason for preferring one to the others, for in most cases, the author's text will be indifferent to all inquiry. Does Tolstoy's text imply that everything true of the actual world is also true, except where it conflicts with it, in *Anna Karenina*? Or only that everything believed true in the society in which it was composed, or in the society in which it was set, is true in the novel? Does William Golding's text imply that everything generally believed true in the prehistoric society in which *The Inheritors* was set, was also true, where it did not conflict with it, in the fiction? Does the text of a novel designed to be published one hundred years after it was composed imply that whatever the audience at that time generally believes about the actual world is also true in the novel (always provided it is consistent with the fictional truths in the novel)?

In the vast majority of cases we cannot answer. But if we cannot answer, the truth or falsity of a great many propositions in fiction is thus undeterminable. Nevertheless, the fact that this is so should not disturb us, for these propositions are usually irrelevant to our appreciation of the fiction. Fiction-makers invite us to participate in an activity of make-believe, so they must indicate what we need to know in order to engage in that activity; but they need not indicate what the activity does not require we know. Small wonder if in fact they do not.

Fictional worlds are thus relatively porous – they have truth-value gaps that the actual world does not, but there is no reason why they should be otherwise. The hypothetical critic's impatient response to the questions we posed earlier, 'Who cares?' is therefore now given a ground that largely vindicates it.

The truth-relevance question

'Beauty is truth, truth beauty,' Keats famously wrote '– that is all ye know on earth, and all ye need to know.'[4] He attributed the words, with poetic licence, to a Grecian urn, but, whatever their provenance, the proposition they express is plainly false. Beauty is no more identical with truth than humanity is with intelligence. But, assuming the poem implies that these two lines are true, what would their actual falsity have to do with the poem's value as literature? 'Nothing at all', some would say. Others would hesitate. 'Don't we praise some literary works for their realism or insight, and censure others for their shallowness or naivete?' they would respond. 'And when we do so, are we not judging them good or bad as literature for reflecting or revealing certain truths, or for failing to reflect or reveal them?' There is some obscurity here as to what precisely is at stake. As with the issue of interpretation, so here, the dispute between the two sides has sometimes generated more heat than light. What is most needed is a cool analysis of the issues that will provide more light than heat.[5]

We said just now: 'Assuming the poem implies that these two lines are true', but is this an assumption we are justified in making? Perhaps not in this case, perhaps the poem takes no stand on the proposition that truth is beauty, but merely imputes it to the urn. Nevertheless, there can be little doubt that many literary works do express, endorse, state or suggest propositions about the actual world that are either true or false (which is why political, religious and moral authorities so often seek to censor literature). Let us say that, when they do so, they *convey* them. They may convey them either by explicitly asserting or by implying them. Carlyle's *French Revolution* (taking it as a work of literature as well as history) conveys by asserting them many true and doubtless some false propositions about events and people in late eighteenth-century France. Dickens's novel *A Tale of Two Cities* conveys, by implying, some true or false propositions about the same place and roughly the same period. George Orwell's *Animal Farm* is a satire implying propositions about some twentieth-century revolutions and the perversion of their ends by unscrupulous dictatorial power-seekers. Aesop's *Fables* and the parables of the New Testament often go further than Orwell, who only implies. The fable of the fox and the grapes and the parable of the prodigal son at first imply the propositions that are their respective morals, and then, at the end, more or less explicitly assert them. (It is not simply propositions that a literary work may imply or suggest. Just as a metaphor may nudge us to see similarities or dissimilarities, so may a work itself nudge us to see them or to see things differently – and not all that we are thus encouraged to see need be propositional. But for the sake of simplicity here, we will consider only propositions.)

How do works of fiction manage to imply propositions about the actual world? The answer to this question was foreshadowed in the previous section. Consider Dickens's *A Tale of Two Cities*. In that work, it is by setting the story in actual eighteenth-century France, and representing fictional characters and events in that setting in the way he does, that Dickens implies that, for instance, the French Revolution involved cruelty and injustice. This kind of implication runs in a different direction from the implications we have just been discussing with respect to what is true *in* fiction. In the previous case, the fact of the novel's being set in eighteenth-century France might (but might not) imply that whatever is true of eighteenth-century France, and compatible with the novel, is also true in the novel. But in the present case, the question is not about what is true *in* the novel, but about whether the novel is true *of* eighteenth-century France. We are not speaking of projecting the actual world onto the fictional, but of projecting the fictional world onto the actual, and the implication itself is not grounded solely in a general principle of communication (e.g. that one should not mislead one's audience), but in a more specific convention about fictional worlds: that they may imply propositions about the actual world. This convention is invoked in Orwell's *Animal Farm*, even though that fiction is not set in the actual world in the way that *A Tale of Two Cities* is; the audience understands from various clues in the text that the farm stands for a type of twentieth-century human society and the animals for typical members of such a society.

Thus the implications that both *A Tale of Two Cities* and *Animal Farm* carry about the actual world are grounded in the convention that fictions may, in their fictional features, convey views about the actual world. 'May', not 'must'; for the convention can be set aside. An 'absurd' fiction might be set in the actual world, yet not imply propositions about it. Dickens or Orwell might have cancelled the implications that their stories carried about actual nineteenth- or twentieth-century societies. Dickens, for instance, might have written a preface disclaiming any intention to represent features of the actual French Revolution in his novel. He would thus have cancelled the implication that the French Revolution involved injustice and cruelty – although it is questionable whether he would have been believed. Orwell might have written a corresponding preface to *Animal Farm* although, again, it is questionable whether he would have been believed. In the same way, someone might tell a joke about some fictional members of a certain group in such a way as to imply that actual members of that group shared the same ludicrous characteristic as the fictional ones – and then add 'But I don't mean that actual members of that group are like that,' and thereby cancel the implication – and it is equally questionable whether *that* disclaimer would be believed. Dickens or Orwell might have cancelled the implications of their works in this way, but their failure to do so leaves the implications about (some aspects of) eighteenth-century France and twentieth-century revolutions intact, and even if they did successfully cancel the implications, their readers would in all probability find that, although the novels did not *imply* them, they did, nevertheless, *suggest* views about the actual world. In the same way, your behaviour can suggest to onlookers that you are upset although not only do you not imply it by what you say, but you actually deny it.

The relevance of truth

Granted that literary works may convey propositions about the actual world, what relevance does the truth or falsity of the propositions conveyed have to the literary value of the work? There are certainly some propositions that a literary work may convey, the truth or falsity of which is irrelevant to our estimation of them as literature. Carlyle's *French Revolution* conveys many propositions, straightforwardly asserted, about precisely who did precisely what precisely when, the truth or falsity of which is irrelevant to a literary assessment of his work. In historical novels it often happens that the author gets some minor detail wrong, so that the work conveys a false proposition, yet the mistake has no bearing on the work's literary value. Suppose, for instance, that Tolstoy's *War and Peace* had conveyed, whether directly by assertion or indirectly by implication, the proposition that there were fifty-one Orthodox churches in Moscow in 1812, whereas in fact there were only fifty; or that Napoleon was five feet two inches tall, whereas in fact he was five feet two and a half. Minor errors like these would surely not affect the literary worth of the novel. So we can say straight off that a few truths or falsities such as these are irrelevant to a work's literary value.

If, however, in the case of an historical novel, the historical figures, places and events are so generally distorted that they bear little relationship to the actual ones, then inevitably the work's status as an historical novel is affected. If Dickens's Paris or Tolstoy's Moscow had borne no relation at all to the actual nineteenth-century Paris and Moscow, either their stories would not have been historical novels at all, in the sense of being fictional narratives set in nonfictional places and situations, or they would have been defective ones. The Paris and Moscow of their works would have been as unreal as the avowedly fictional characters they placed in them.

What about the truth or falsity of propositions that express the theme or moral of a fictional work? Some of Alexander Solzhenitsyn's novels imply that Stalinist Russia was a brutal police state, while Orwell's *Animal Farm*, we noted earlier, implies propositions about the course of certain types of twentieth-century revolutions, and Thomas Hardy's works are often said (let us suppose truly) to imply a pessimistic view of human life. Should we think less highly of these works as literature if we know or believe the views they imply are false? Should we think more highly of them if we know or believe the views implied are true?

It seems that we should distinguish between explicitly asserted and fictionally implied views here. As we saw just now, if Carlyle in his *French Revolution* had got some main facts about the period wrong, when he could have got them right, or had generally put an unreasonably false interpretation on them, that would surely have made his book poorer as history; but it would not have made it poorer as literature. For when we consider a work of history as literature, we are not concerned with the quality of its historical research – Carlyle's qualities as a historian are not literary qualities. Similarly, if Lucretius, in his *On the Nature of Things*, had made inaccurate assertions, by the standards of his time, about the physical world, that would have shown he did not know much contemporary science, not that he was a bad poet. Probably we should find both works less valuable as a whole if they were poor history or poor science; for what we think are poor history and poor science are generally, in themselves, less interesting than good history and good science. But we should not then be judging the works from a literary point of view.

When we turn to fictional works, however, in which a view about the world is not directly asserted on the basis of evidence, but implied by the fiction itself, different considerations seem to apply. For we are not now dealing with the details of historical or scientific research, but with a general view of the world or some aspects of it as implied by the nature of an imaginative representation of it. Solzhenitsyn's *One Day in the Life of Ivan Denisovich* implies by means of its fictional narrative that Stalinist Russia was in some ways a brutal police state. In this way it presents a fictional portrait of the actual world. One of the dimensions in which we assess such a portrait as a work of fiction is its accuracy to the world it thus portrays. If we thought the propositions it implied about Stalinist Russia were entirely false, we would think less highly of the novel, just as we would think less highly of a painter's portrait of a person if it in no way resembled that person. Both works might be excellent in other ways, but in that one way they would fail. If there were no features of actual twentieth-century society, such as Orwell implied there were in *Animal Farm*, his work would be diminished as a satire (just as a cartoonist's caricature of a politician is defective if

the politician lacks the features which the cartoonist exaggerates and empha-
sises). If Hardy's pessimism is groundless, the works implying it are less
good than they would be if it were not, for they would imply a one-sided or
distorted view of the actual world. This does not mean, we said, that the
works would thereby become failures, for they might be good in other ways,
but they would be flawed in the same way that portraits or caricatures are
flawed if their subjects wholly lack the features attributed to them. Thus,
what makes Solzhenitsyn a good novelist is not merely that his representation of Stalinist Russia as a brutal police state was generally correct, but
also his ability to make in his stories a convincing portrayal of people living
under such a state, whether or not it was true to the actual world. What
makes Hardy a good novelist is not merely his perception – if perception it is
– of the relentless disappointments of human endeavours, but also his
ability, among other things, to present interesting, sympathetic and
convincing characters in doomed situations, whether or not the actual world
is as his novels imply it is. In Graham Greene's novel *It's A Battlefield*, a
gloomy and negative view is implied of the social and political situation in
London in the 1930s. The truth or falsity of that view – or our perception of
it as true or false – is one, but it is not the only, nor even perhaps, the major,
factor in our assessment of the novel's success. Perhaps the moral of Aesop's
fable of the fox and the grapes is false. That would mean it was a worse fable
than it would have been if it had drawn our attention to something that was
true; but it would not mean the fable was a complete failure. For what may
remain in all these cases is that the works present situations and characters
in their fictions which are striking and interesting in many other ways.

We have been speaking of fiction, but what we have been saying applies to
figures of speech like metaphors and similes, too, which are equally at home
in or out of fiction. Just as we distinguish between the characterisation, plot,
imagery, etc. of a novel and the propositions which the work, by means of
those features, may come to imply, so we can distinguish between the
vivacity and force of a simile or metaphor and the truth of what it asserts or
suggests. The aptness of such figures is a matter of the fit of what they
assert or suggest to the things they suggest or assert them about. That is as
relevant to their value as similes or metaphors as is the truth of the propositions Orwell's *Animal Farm* implies to the value of the satire in which they
are conveyed. 'How apt!' and 'How true!' when said of a metaphor or simile,
are remarks as integral to a proper evaluation of those figures as they would
be to a literary evaluation of *Animal Farm* if uttered about the views on
revolutions and dictators which the novel implies. 'How striking!' or 'How
vivid!', however, are also integral to their evaluation – just as they would be
if uttered about the fictional descriptions by means of which Orwell implied
the views that are conveyed in *Animal Farm*.

We have been dealing with the propositions implied by the tenor or character of literary works, but that is not the only place in which we can find

that truth is relevant to literary value. Indeed, when we look elsewhere, we see that there are plenty of critical spaces where truth is relevant. Suppose it were established, for instance, that the view that Solzhenitsyn's works imply of Stalinist Russia was completely false, and that Russia at that time was as its propagandists portrayed it, a workers' paradise. That would certainly be a flaw in Solzhenitsyn's work but, as we have just noted, it would not necessarily show he was a poor novelist. He might still be a good novelist if his works were impressive for their imaginative force, their interesting and stimulating themes, their convincing characterisation, their capacity to involve us emotionally in the fate of their characters. Similarly (although, since portraiture is more like biography than it is like fiction, analogies with painting cannot be taken too far), if Rembrandt's self-portrait of 1660 does not resemble him at all, it is still a good painting because of its representation of mood, character, texture, colour, shape, light and shade, etc.

To return to Solzhenitsyn: what does the hypothetical verdict on his work which we have just suggested reveal about our critical criteria? Surely, for such a verdict to be justified, the development of the plot must be credible, the characters believable and interesting, their language plausible, their fates convincing. ... In other words, it must be true (or, at any rate, we must believe it is – a qualification that does not affect the issue) that things like that *could* happen to people like that, who *would* act and speak like that in that kind of situation from those kinds of motives. ... Our praise of the psychological insight or perception of Solzhenitsyn would then be based on what we considered to be the probable behaviour, thoughts and feelings of real people faced with situations like those represented in the fictional world of the novel, not on the features of Stalinist Russia as Solzhenitsyn implied they were. On the other hand, our dissatisfaction with a work of this genre is often due to our belief in the probability that people would not actually behave as they are fictionally represented as acting in the novel. 'But someone like that who had undergone that would not act in that way,' we say; or 'But that's completely out of character'; or 'That character is lifeless and unconvincing'. If our disbelief in the probability is justified, that is indeed a ground for dispraise (although it might not be so in the case of a different kind of work – say, a surreal or deliberately absurd one). This, perhaps, is the truth that lies behind Aristotle's remarks in *The Poetics*, that poetry is 'more philosophical than history, in that history says what did happen, poetry the kind of thing that would happen'.[6] It is our conception of what is in general likely to be the case ('the kind of thing that would happen') that we bring with us to such works and which, if correct, justifies some of our critical reactions to them.

The fact that literary works play against the background of our beliefs in this way does not mean, we should add, that the scope of literature is in this respect limited to merely reflecting what we are already fully conscious of. It may draw things to our attention that we had not previously considered (just as a metaphor may). Nevertheless, our judgement of what it thus draws to our attention will be controlled, in this sphere, by what we believe to be probable. Huck's soliloquy on the raft, in Mark Twain's *The Adventures of Huckleberry Finn*, about whether or not he should turn in his companion, the runaway slave, Jim, has been described as 'a brilliant depiction of moral struggle'.[7] If it is so, it is because it represents moral struggle as (we believe) it probably would have been for someone in the actual world who was relevantly like Huck, and that may be something that we have not seriously considered before, something that we are brought to realise only as we read the passage; such a realisation can be as revelatory as can the recognition of the truth of some proposition which a work as a whole implies.

Literature and morality

We have seen how literature can state or imply various propositions. This is one way in which it may become liable to censorship, for the propositions may be uncongenial to political, moral or religious orthodoxy. But literature may also incur censorship simply because of the nature of what it portrays, irrespective of the propositions that it conveys about it. Some authorities may consider a work objectionable because it contains material too shocking to be published, for instance (say, the description of a gruesome murder or accident), even though the relevant proposition implicitly conveyed by the work may be the innocuous one that murder is evil or drunken driving is dangerous. As many societies have censorship, in the form of laws penalising obscene, blasphemous and politically or morally subversive publications, the whole question of the relationship of morality (religious and secular) and literature deserves at least a brief examination. One thing that is necessary here is the explosion of some myths.

One myth concerns the sense in which works of fiction can on occasion be said to convey moral, political or religious (or any other) truths. Sometimes fictional works of literature do set out to convey such supposed truths, and sometimes they succeed. Tolstoy's *Resurrection* is a novel which implies the truth of certain Christian religious and moral views. Suppose, for the sake of argument, that those views are true. A critic might be tempted to say that the novel, in its characterisation and development, had *shown* they were true. This would be wrong, as the discussion of the previous section has implied. The novel may well imply that the views are true, and do so very forcefully, but it cannot itself authenticate the views it conveys – whether the view is a sound one depends on what the (moral and religious) facts are, not on how the author's fiction represents them. So, while fictional literature may imply such truths, it cannot guarantee them. This does not mean, of course, that we cannot gather truths from fiction, only that they are not *shown* to be truths by virtue of being persuasively conveyed in a novel, story, poem, film or play. In this sense, claims that fiction has some kind of special route to moral (or any other) truth must be rejected as fanciful.

The situation with nonfictional works, however, is not the same. Donne's *Sermons* convey various Christian religious-moral views, too, but more by means of argument than by fictional representation. If Donne's arguments were good enough, they might prove the views were true. A work of fiction can never do that. It works by imaginative suggestion, not logic, as Plato indistinctly recognised in *The Republic*, although he had no word for imagination. Deeply mistrustful of ordinary people's rational abilities, and considering that they would often be seduced by literary works into taking propositions conveyed by them as true when they were not, and into acting on them accordingly, Plato saw grounds for censorship of much literature (and indeed most art) in an ideal state.[8] The same sort of reasoning has been used to justify censorship ever since. However, whatever might be said for it in some cases, such reasoning loses a good deal of its bite when the common people are reasonably educated and intelligent, a possibility which Plato apparently did not envisage.

Another myth concerning morality (in its broadest sense) and literature is that works of literature can be moral or immoral in themselves. This is a confusion. It may be moral or immoral, under certain circumstances, to compose a work, as it might perhaps be argued that Gauguin acted immorally in leaving his family and going off to paint. Surely the suffering caused to others by engaging in the composition of a work might sometimes outweigh the benefit thereby obtained. A pretty, but minor, sonnet would scarcely justify letting one's family starve. But this is not to say that the sonnet itself is immoral – it is the composing of it under those circumstances that is morally bad, not the thing composed. Again, it might be morally wrong to publish a work, because of the bad effects that publishing it would have, but that would not mean that the thing published was in itself morally bad. A case can be made for saying that, if it had been known in advance how many deaths and how much other suffering would ensue upon the publication of Salman Rushdie's *Satanic Verses*,[9] it would have been wrong to publish it. (Such a case would, of course, have to confront the reply that the benefits of maintaining freedom of thought and expression outweighed the suffering consequent upon publishing the work.) But even if the argument were accepted, it would not follow that the book itself was morally bad. What was bad would have been the act of publishing it, not what was published. In the same way it might also be said that it was wrong for someone to read a work (of pornography, say) which he knew might incite him to rape. But again the moral fault would be in the person reading the work, or in the publishing of it, not in the work read or published.

Can a work of literature, say of pornography, not be immoral in itself, then? It does not seem so. A description, however produced, whether fictional or factual, unlike the producer or the producing, cannot in itself be the subject of moral predicates. Consider a film of a violent crime, made by a security video-camera that happened to be operating at the scene. The act was morally bad, but the film which recorded it was neither morally bad nor morally good. The same is true of an unvarnished newspaper report of what happened in the crime. And so, surely, must it be when we consider a fictional description of a crime just like the actual one: because of the effects it had, the description should perhaps not have been written or published or read, but the description in itself can only be as morally neutral as the security video film. When, therefore, censors, or others, condemn a work for being immoral, it should not be the work that, rightly or wrongly, they castigate, but, usually, its publication. It does not make sense to ascribe moral predicates to sentences or propositions. Those predicates can be ascribed only to actions and agents. Sentences and propositions, as opposed to utterings or readings of them, or their utterers or readers, are neither.

As to the case for or against censorship in some form or other, the problem is not the complexity or obscurity of the principles involved, for they are fairly simple and clear. There is the right to freedom of expression and there is the right of others not to be harmed by the exercise of that right. The difficulty lies in applying the principles to particular cases in which the circumstances are uncertain or messy. How highly should we rank freedom of expression in a case where those exposed to it are likely to be offended by the expression of certain views? Or where the mere knowledge of the material's availability offends a certain section of the community? Or where the right is secured for some people at the expense of the lives or welfare of others?

These issues belong more to the province of social philosophy than to that of the philosophy of literature, so we shall not pursue them further here.[10] But we should say something about the relevance of the moral views a work may convey to the literary value of the work itself. Just as, following Keats, we asked whether truth was relevant to beauty, so we may ask whether goodness is.

Does the correctness or otherwise of the moral or political views conveyed by a work affect the work's literary value? It seems that it does, in the same way that the nonmoral implications of a work do. Leni Riefenstahl's *Triumph of the Will* is a film (let us ignore the fact – irrelevant here – that it is not a literary work) which is said to have conveyed by implying it the view that Nazism was a glorious and heroic movement, and hence to have encouraged people at the time it was first shown to support Nazism. Let us suppose this is so, and also – which is rather harder – suppose that the imagery, etc. which conveyed that view was not crass and bombastic but, on the contrary, subtle and eloquent. Then the falsity of the moral-political view it conveyed would affect its value as a film, just as, if the propositions that Orwell's *Animal Farm* implied about twentieth-century society had been false, that would have affected the novel's value as a satire.

And for the same reason: the view of the world implied would be a false and distorted one. That would not mean, however, that the film was in *every* way a failure. In some cases, a work's false moral implications might be offset by its other qualities, particularly if those implications were not outrageously distorted. For there is a range of dimensions in which we assess literary works, and hence we might admire a work for some things while detesting it for others. Baudelaire's poem *Les Bijoux* has been said to convey morally unacceptable (sexist) attitudes towards women[11] but, if it does, while that means it is a less good poem than it might have been, for it implies a morally distorted view of the world, it does not follow that it is not still a good poem, even though it may well affect our ability to see it as one. We noticed that Solzhenitsyn's novels might have conveyed false views about Stalinist Russia (although in general they did not), and yet have been good novels because of the perceptive characterisation and moving, unsentimental descriptions of the fictional persons and events presented in the novels. So it is with morality: an author might present perceptive characterisations and moving, unsentimental descriptions of fictional persons while conveying the view that a moral position or political ideology was right when in fact it was wrong. That would affect the literary value of the work, but the work might still, on balance, be a good one despite that. This will usually be so only where the moral or political view implied is not outrageous. When a work conveys a grossly distorted view, it generally does so in a crass and crude manner, so that it is deeply defective in other ways, as well as implying false moral or political views.

Conclusion

It seems that truth in fictional worlds is largely underdetermined, and that truth to the actual world is sometimes relevant to literary value, whether the truth is moral or nonmoral. In discussing these questions, however, we have been assuming that there is such a thing as literary value. That raises another question: Are judgements of literary value objective, subjective, or relative to a culture, society or time? We shall take up this question in the next chapter.

9

LITERARY APPRAISALS

Prologue

In a much quoted phrase, which was adopted as the title of one contemporary critic's book, T. S. Eliot described the critical endeavour as 'the common pursuit of true judgement'.[1] This seems to presuppose that there is an objectively correct, or true, judgement to be achieved, or at least aimed at, in that common, if sometimes contentious, pursuit. The not uncommon failure to agree as to what this judgement is, particularly where the quarry is a value judgement or appraisal as opposed to an interpretative or historical one, may be one reason why critics now tend to adopt a less objectivist stance. Another is almost certainly the diffusion of Deconstructionists' and like-minded theorists' arguments through university literature departments.[2]

There are three positions that can be adopted on this issue, which are not always defined in the same way, but which I shall characterise as follows:

- *Objectivism*: the view apparently implied by Eliot's remark, that literary value judgements are unqualifiedly correct or mistaken, regardless of whether anyone actually thinks they are.
- *Relativism*: the view that such judgements are correct or mistaken only relative to a culture or cultural group (or 'subculture'), so that saying a work is good is saying that it is good in, or relative to, a certain (sub) culture.
- *Subjectivism*: the view that no such judgement is either correct or mistaken at all (not even relative to a culture), and that, rather than describing some feature of the thing judged, literary 'judgements' arise from, express or report only an attitude towards it.

The characterisation I have just given of these positions may be described as broadly metaphysical. It addresses the issue of whether literary appraisals can be true or false, and questions about what *can* be true or false are often regarded as metaphysical questions. Another characterisation of the different positions may be called epistemological. It is that subjective judgements cannot be 'shown' to be right or wrong, whereas objective judgements can, while relativistic judgements can be shown to be so only in relation to some cultural group. I call this epistemological because it is concerned with whether it can be shown (known) that a certain judgement is right or wrong, true or false. A third characterisation of objectivism is specifically ontological. It is that aesthetic, hence literary, values are features of the works themselves, not in any way dependent on the activities or judgements of those who read or hear them, a claim that both subjectivism and relativism, on this characterisation, would deny. While there are connections between all these ways of characterising the three positions, there are also differences, so that they yield slightly different consequences. Nevertheless, the connections are so close that it is unlikely that an argument for objectivism, say, under one characterisation would not offer some support to it under another. It will be enough here to consider the issue only as it is presented under the first characterisation.[3]

Relativism

Relativism seems to be both the most popular and the most problematic of these positions. There is first of all a certain haziness as to what constitutes the culture or subculture to which value judgements are supposed to be relative. What are the boundaries of these groups, how are they defined? Is there French culture only, or French nineteenth-century culture, too? Or early, mid- and late nineteenth-century French culture as well (or instead)? If the last, then is there also early, mid- and late early nineteenth-century French culture, etc.? How do we distinguish between a culture and a subculture?

An associated problem is how to account for opposed judgements within a cultural group. It sometimes – indeed quite often – happens that opposed judgements are made about the same work by different critics from the same culture at the same time. When there are thus two opposed judgements within the same culture, are both right relative to the culture? Or should we say that each is right relative to its own subculture? But surely mere disagreement of judgements would not entail that there were two cultural groups involved, so that the members of a cultural group would by definition be homogeneous and always make the same judgements. How will the relativist account for changing judgements within the same cultural group, which also sometimes plainly happens – or is that, too, by definition, indicative of a change of culture? Relativism's inability or omission, at least, to answer such questions clearly renders it vague and liable to degenerate into the view that the 'cultural group' with respect to which judgements are relative is ultimately the individual making the judgement at the time he is making it.[4]

One argument that is commonly offered in support of relativism is unconvincing. It is that where different cultural groups (however we decide what they are) have opposing value judgements, there is no way to determine which is correct; from which the conclusion is drawn that each judgement is correct relative to its group. This argument is fallacious. Even if we accept the premise that there is no way of determining which of differing judgements between groups is right, it does not follow that each is right relative to its own cultural group. Perhaps one is right although it cannot be shown to be so; or perhaps all are wrong; or perhaps, as some subjectivists say, there cannot be any right (or wrong) where there is no possibility of showing it to be so – a position which itself, of course, needs argument to support it. So the relativist's argument needs to be strengthened here, although it is not clear where the strength is going to come from.

The failure of relativists to answer such questions as these satisfactorily makes it difficult to resist the suspicion that at bottom they have identified 'X is *judged* good in culture C' with 'X *is* good in culture C' – two sentences with apparently quite different meanings. If they offer the first as the reason for believing the second, the suspicion that they have indeed identified the two becomes stronger. For, of course, if the two sentences had the same meaning, we could legitimately infer the second from the first. But the trouble is, relativists have given us no reason to think they do have the same meaning.

Subjectivism, while not without its difficulties, is an easier thesis to defend. But since both subjectivism and relativism agree in rejecting objectivism, it is best to take this question as the great divide, and make that the focus of our discussion. Are literary appraisals objective or not? Once we have settled that, or even in the course of settling it, we shall perhaps become clearer about subjectivism. But we cannot hope to settle it without examining the various kinds of appraisal that the critic, and, for that matter, each of us when in critical mode, actually makes. An unexpected consequence of thus analysing literary appraisals, and aesthetic appraisals generally, is that we are led to wonder whether the question of their objectivity is as important as heavily engaged disputants seem inclined to suppose.

Terms of appraisal: Kant's analysis

We make many different kinds of appraisals of literary works, as we do of paintings, sculpture, music, food, wine, people, actions and just about everything else. Sometimes we pass a general verdict that the work is good or bad, at other times we commend or discommend some particular aspect of the work – saying it is elegant or crude, sentimental or moving, restrained or colourless, profound or portentous, eloquent or bombastic. Some of these more specific appraisals are characteristically offered as reasons for the overall verdict: 'It's bad because it's portentous,' or 'It's good because it's so restrained.' Whether general or specific, it is notorious that people tend to disagree more about whether terms of appraisal apply to a given work than they do about whether such expressions as 'in verse', 'in prose', 'having an irregular metre', 'containing half-rhymes', 'highly figurative', 'having a complicated plot', 'dealing with death or love', etc. do, although there can be disagreement about these, too. What is the explanation of this difference? How do these appraisals come to be made at all?

Kant held that judgements that a particular thing is beautiful are made in the course, or as the result, of the judging subject's perceiving or experiencing the thing judged. (It is worth recalling here that 'aesthetic' comes from the Greek word for perception.) He claimed that, although they claimed universal validity, such judgements were grounded solely in the feeling of pleasure that arose from the individual subject's perceiving.[5] He set himself to explain how such judgements could be justified. The considerable detail in which Kant worked out this account need not concern us here, but, applying it to the specific case of literature, one thing that would follow from his theory is that, whatever one had been told about a literary work, one would not in fact judge it aesthetically (literarily) except in or as a result of experiencing (reading, hearing, or, in the case of plays or films, seeing) it.

Kant's view, which was developed partly from those held by a number of eighteenth-century thinkers, seems both important and correct on that point. An aesthetic, and hence a literary, appraisal is grounded in the sense of satisfaction or dissatisfaction that the appraiser feels while, or as a direct result of, apprehending the work. (Kant, we have seen, used 'pleasure' not 'satisfaction', but either term will do equally well.) Someone who is acquainted with the plot of *King Lear*, even in great detail, but has neither read nor seen a performance of it, may well declare either that the play is boring or that it is gripping, but, while he is saying something about the play, he is not, strictly, passing an aesthetic (literary) judgement on it; if anything, he is predicting what aesthetic judgement he would make if he actually did see or read it. (If someone wishes to protest that he is making an aesthetic judgement, but one that he is not entitled to make, I will not object. The point transcends terminology: such a judgement can be described as either not an aesthetic judgement or not a proper aesthetic judgement.) This distinguishes appraisals from other types of literary judgement. Someone who is given a full and accurate description of the metrical scheme of a poem or of the plot of a novel does not need to read them in order to say whether the poem has an irregular metre or whether the novel deals with love or death; he has the necessary information already.

In this respect, aesthetic judgements are different from moral ones, too, a point that should make us wary of assuming, as some do, that there is an exact analogy between the two types of judgement. From a relevantly full description of an action, we can make a (proper) moral judgement about it, and witnessing the action would make no difference to our judgement of its rightness or wrongness, unless it showed us that the description was in some way false. I do not need to *see* a man torturing another person for the sole

127

reason that it gives him pleasure to do so, before I can judge that his action is wrong; *knowing* that is what his action was is sufficient. That is because the description of the action already shows that it infringes the moral principle that one should not cause severe pain to others solely for one's own pleasure. An equally full description of the plot of *King Lear*, by contrast, is aesthetically impotent; while it may enable us to pronounce moral judgements on the actions portrayed, it cannot enable us to pronounce (proper) aesthetic judgements on the portrayal itself. That depends on what sense of satisfaction or dissatisfaction seeing or reading the play arouses in us. 'How can you judge the play without seeing or reading it?' must be a valid reproach. 'How can you judge someone's action without witnessing it?' need not be.

It is because literary and other aesthetic appraisals are grounded in a sense of satisfaction or dissatisfaction in respect of the features apprehended in experiencing the work that we generally find it harder to settle disagreements about judgements such as: 'This novel is mannered', or 'This play is elegantly constructed', than we do to settle disagreements about such judgements as: 'This novel deals with love or death', or 'This play is in verse' – judgements that are not appraisals of the work's value. For the latter, as we noticed, can be made on the basis of a relevant description of the work, and so are open to demonstration, while the former, being grounded only in a sense of satisfaction or dissatisfaction in apprehending the work, are not.

Not only do we find it harder to settle such disagreements but there are generally more of them. That there are more disagreements about them than about other judgements shows nothing in itself as to their subjectivity or objectivity. But that the judgement arises from an individual's satisfaction or dissatisfaction regarding the features apprehended does. For if this is the case, it seems that one's judgement, in so far as it is grounded in one's satisfaction or otherwise, can no more be either correct or mistaken than one's liking red wine or white wine can be. Kant, holding that 'judgements of the beautiful' claim universal validity, sought to avoid this conclusion by arguing that such judgements related to purely formal features in an object and that those features would engage only formal features of our mental faculties (that is, the way our mental faculties worked together in the process of perception, not the various data presented for them to work on). The smooth functioning of those faculties (which he called the imagination and the understanding) in the activity of perceiving objects which happened to be peculiarly suited to the manner of the faculties' operation, he thought, gave rise to the particular pleasure which grounds the judgement of the beautiful. He held that these mental features, unlike our temperaments, could be presumed not to vary between individuals; for if they did vary, we would not be able to communicate with each other, as we evidently do.[6] Hence they could justifiably claim universal validity, even though they could never be proved correct or incorrect.

It follows from this that, according to Kant, the form and structure of a rose or of a tune could give rise to an aesthetic judgement, but the yellow colour of the petal could not, nor could the reedy tone of the oboe playing the tune. The reasons why we feel pleasure in perceiving one colour rather than another, or one tone rather than another, he thought, are individually variable; so expressions of such pleasure, not being entitled to claim universal validity, could not be aesthetic judgements.[7] However, he considered that the reasons why we feel pleasure in perceiving one *form* rather than another are not individually variable; they relate to the structure of the mind itself, which, if we succeed in communicating with each other, must be the same in all of us. The first kind of judgement is therefore in his view merely psychological, while the second is aesthetic. In this way he sought to provide a vindication of that demand for universal validity which he maintained is made by a judgement that something is beautiful, grounded though it is only in a feeling of pleasure or satisfaction.

Kant's mistake

We should note that Kant is not making the strong claim that aesthetic judgements are objective – at least in the sense that they can be demonstrated to be correct – but the weaker one that they can justifiably claim universal validity. Nevertheless, for all its ingenuity, his is an implausible solution to an unreal problem, committing us as it does to the unconvincing conclusion that sentences such as 'Titian's rust reds are gorgeous', or 'Fournier's cello tone was richer than Tortelier's', are not aesthetic judgements. There are four reasons why Kant's view should be rejected.

The first we have just alluded to: not all our aesthetic judgements are formal in the sense Kant defines. The hypothetical judgements about Titian and Fournier just cited would surely be genuine aesthetic judgements, even though they were not grounded in feelings of satisfaction ensuing on the apprehension of any 'formal' features of anything or on the relation between the object apprehended and what Kant calls the faculties of imagination and understanding.

The second concerns the view that the aesthetic judgement *justifiably* demands universal assent or validity. This carries with it the claims that people judging solely on the formal grounds Kant specifies would all make the same judgement and that, if two judgements disagreed, at least one of them must be mistaken. (Although Kant does not say that aesthetic judgements are objective, this second claim certainly comes as close as may be to saying that, in the sense in which we have defined the term, they are.) Neither of these claims is justified. For even if we granted what Kant requires of an aesthetic judgement, that everyone would indeed feel satisfaction at the interaction of the formal features of a perceived object with the formal features of the perceiving mind (and there is much to question here), there is no particular reason to think they must all feel just the same *quality* of satisfaction to just the same *degree*. The formal relations between our mental faculties might be sufficiently similar for human communication to take place, as Kant postulated, while also being sufficiently different to allow variations between individuals, so that some felt more, or less, satisfaction at the smooth working of the faculties than others, or satisfaction of a slightly different kind. But if so, the problem Kant sought to avoid, that individual temperaments vary as far as the mind's nonformal features go, would reappear here – they might vary as far as its formal features go, too. Hence, judgements made solely on such formal grounds need not agree, and a difference in such judgements would not show that at least one of them was mistaken.

Third, Kant ignores the heterogeneous variety of aesthetic, hence of literary, judgements. He speaks of our judging something beautiful, as if we made only one kind of aesthetic judgement.[8] But our literary, or aesthetic, judgements are many and multifarious, and it is misleading to assimilate them all with each other. Moreover, the way in which we make them indicates that most are neither wholly subjective nor wholly objective. I shall develop this point further in the next section.

Finally, there are other, more plausible, explanations of why, in so far as they do, aesthetic judgements 'claim universal validity'. I shall take up this point in the next but one section.

Objective and subjective conditions

Consider some of the expressions we have already mentioned: 'elegant', 'crude'; 'sentimental'. 'moving;' 'profound', 'portentous;' 'eloquent', 'bombastic'. These are pairs of contrasting terms, each member of which is characteristically used to make a favourable or adverse judgement. To say that a story in *Just Seventeen* is sentimental is to dispraise it, to say that it is moving is to praise it. To call Henry's rallying 'Crispian Day' speech in Shakespeare's *Henry The Fifth*[9] eloquent is to praise it, to call it bombastic is to dispraise it. This hardly needs saying. But in making these appraisals we are not just offering general praise or dispraise, or expressing merely a general sense of satisfaction or dissatisfaction. For that, the words 'good' or 'bad' would have done – words we often use, in aesthetic contexts, to give a verdict on the basis of a sense of overall satisfaction or dissatisfaction in the experiencing of something. (Kant perhaps thought of the judgement that something was beautiful as such a general kind of judgement.) These expressions are more specific than 'good' or 'bad', and their specificity is connected with the conditions of their application.[10] There are features that a work must have in order to qualify for these terms, such that, while their presence does not render the application of the term correct, their absence does render it incorrect.[11] The terms are used to praise or dispraise the work *with respect to* those features. Both a sentimental and a moving story must express or evoke emotion. So a work that does not express or evoke emotion at all cannot be either sentimental or moving, and someone who claimed it was one or the other would therefore be mistaken.

So far, the question is an objective one: independently of anyone's judgement, a work that lacked those qualities would be neither sentimental nor moving. But while the presence of these features is thus a necessary condition for the application of such terms, it is not a sufficient one, and it is here that the subjective element of the judgement comes into play. The judgement that the novel is sentimental or the speech eloquent, if made on relevant grounds, is based on the audience's feeling of dissatisfaction or satisfaction in apprehending the relevant features of the work. One reader may feel satisfaction in the apprehension of just those emotion-related features of the work in the apprehension of which another may feel no satisfaction or positive dissatisfaction. Or they may both feel satisfaction, but of different degrees: one more, one less. Or they may even feel exactly the same satisfaction to exactly the same degree (although it is hard to see how we might find that out). But whatever the situation, there is ultimately no independent fact of the matter which would render any of these judgements right or wrong. For, being grounded in feelings of satisfaction or dissatisfaction, there is no basis for a claim to universal validity (and that would be so even if we discovered there was universal *concurrence*).

In this respect, they are of the same kind as judgements about wine. Some theorists have ridiculed the idea that there can be an analogy between purely gustatory judgements and aesthetic ones, feeling, perhaps, that the satisfactions we derive from the arts are far too grand, refined and complex to be compared with those we get from wine-bibbing. But, while those satisfactions do, indeed, relate to different needs and desires, and are typically more grand, refined and complex, if both are grounded in a sense of satisfaction in experiencing certain objects, it is hard to see the reason for the ridicule. The argument runs on the form of the judgement, not its content.

That such judgements are, in the qualified manner just suggested, subjective judgements does not mean that there can be no dispute about them. For a judgement, say, that Henry's 'Crispian Day' speech is eloquent, or that it is bombastic, may be made because the judge has neglected some aspect of the work, and hence is not making an informed judgement. To the extent that it ignored that aspect of the work, the judgement would be defective – as would a judgement about wine which took no account of the presence of some relevant vinous feature. Here we are in the realm of the objective – regardless of whether anyone recognises it, either the feature is there or it is not. But where there is no such failure, whether judgements concur or not, there is no question in either literary or wine appraisals of being right or wrong. So far as appraisals are grounded *only* in each appraiser's satisfaction or dissatisfaction in the apprehension of the same relevant features of the object appraised, thus far there is no independent fact of the matter and the appraisal is subjective.

We noted earlier that a second characterisation of 'objective' was that where there was no way of showing a judgement was right or wrong, the judgement was not objective, but subjective. This view rests on the assumption that it is meaningless to talk of right or wrong judgements when there is no way of showing which is which. (Hence this view is often offered, not as a characterisation of subjectivism, but as an argument for it.) Let us assume, although it is contestable, that this assumption is correct. By this criterion also, the appraisals we have been considering are not objective. Whether or not there is a difference of judgement (after any misunderstandings or misperceptions have been corrected), it cannot be *shown* that such judgements are either correct or incorrect. Thus two people can agree, and be right, about the presence of emotion-related features in a story, but differ irremediably as to whether that makes the story sentimental or not, and there is no way to show that one of them is right. Or they can agree, and be right, about the meaning, imagery and force of Henry's Crispian Day speech, and also agree about whether it is eloquent or bombastic, and again there is no way of showing they are right or wrong, as opposed to coinciding in their judgements. Contrast this with agreement or disagreement over whether a work is in verse or not, whether Henry's speech is made in Act III or Act IV, or whether or not it evinces or elicits emotion at all. While there are sometimes borderline cases which cannot be decided, in most cases simple observation or understanding the meaning of the words in the work will suffice to settle the issue; for here there *is* a way of showing that a view is right or wrong.

Recall, now, the third, ontological, characterisation of objectivisim we gave. This was that literary values were features of literary works which were in no way dependent on the activities of people who appraised them. That view, too, would be affected by the argument I have put forward here. For if there is no possibility of being right or wrong about some literary appraisals, or if it is impossible to show one is right and the other wrong, the view that literary values are features of the works themselves, independent of people's judgements of them, loses much of its plausibility. If there were such features, surely we should expect to be able to discover them and show that judgements about them were either correct or mistaken, as we can show judgements about other features of the work (its being in verse or its dealing with love or death) are. The most likely explanation of why we could not show appraisals of a work were right or wrong would be that there simply was no objective feature of the work there to *make* the appraisals right or wrong.

Objectification of aesthetic attitudes

We have sketched a qualifiedly subjective position, which I think is the most plausible one to adopt for the kind of appraisals we have been discussing. But we have not developed it in detail. We have not, for instance, accommodated the fact that (moral or nonmoral) truth may be a factor in our overall appraisals, a fact, if it is one, which appears to introduce an objective element which the appraisals we have been considering lack. Nor have we defended the position we have sketched as it would need to be defended in order to make it fully convincing. To do these things would require another book. But we should notice how we might answer one query which such a position usually provokes. The query is this: if there is this subjective element in our employment of the literary appraisal terms we have discussed, how does it happen that people argue about their application, instead of accepting, as in the case of differing tastes in wine, that neither is right or wrong? Why, in Kant's formulation, do we claim universal validity for judgements that are grounded in a subjective sense of pleasure or displeasure? In so far as we do make this demand (and it is not clear that we all do, or do all the time), part of the reason has already been given; there is an objective element in most such appraisal terms – the necessary conditions for their application – that permits correction if they are applied when those conditions are not satisfied. As we have noticed, some appraisals are doubtless flawed by carelessness or misapprehension. An emotionless play cannot be either sentimental or moving. A poem consisting of monosyllabic guttural English words and describing fully and realistically a man bludgeoning an infant to death cannot be either gracefully restrained or self-consciously pretty. A judgement that *King Lear* as a whole is bombastic that was based on a reading of a few scenes only would be flawed – if, indeed, we counted it as a proper aesthetic judgement at all. Sometimes, however, though the conditions are satisfied, disagreement remains. We may agree on the metrical and rhyming scheme of a sonnet, for instance, and on what the words mean and suggest, yet one of us finds the poem graceful while the other does not. We agree that the play evokes or expresses emotion, but one of us finds it sentimental while the other does not – or even finds it deeply moving instead. Why do we sometimes seek to persuade each other to see it our way?

Part of the answer now may be that we want others to be like us. If Joan enjoyed what she experienced as the elegance of the poem, then she may well want her friend Hilda to enjoy it too, for that tends to unite them. So she tries to get Hilda to see the poem her way. And this reflects something else; we often care more about people's aesthetic than we do about their gustatory reactions – we rarely try to get others to acquire our taste for white as opposed to red wine or for rabbit as opposed to chicken. Naturally so, for our taste in art can both involve and expose us in ways that our taste in food or drink do not.[12] It is uncomfortable to learn that what you were moved by another thinks is merely sentimental, for sentimentality is a shallow or irrational form of feeling, and even if we do not see that we are sentimental, the implied charge that we are so disquiets us. The more other people's aesthetic judgements diverge, in some cases, from our own, the less we understand and can sympathise with them. But that does not mean that our judgements are objective.

Another part of the answer is that we have a tendency to objectify our preferences. This is sometimes so even in the case of food and drink preferences, but is even more so in the case of aesthetic ones.[13] We typically say that ice cream is nice because we like it ourselves, and that *King Lear* is moving because we are moved by it ourselves. In both cases, however, the epithet goes beyond the individual attitudes that typically give rise to them. 'Nice' and 'moving' have built into them that claim to universal validity to which Kant drew attention with respect to judgements of the beautiful. In saying the ice cream is nice and the play is moving, we are typically claiming more than that *we* like ice cream or that *we* are moved by the play. We are typically (though probably not always) claiming that others should like ice cream or be moved by the play, too: that is, that people are mistaken if they do or are not. In other words, we have *objectified* our individual attitudes, treating them as though they could be correct or mistaken in the same way that attributions of being made with vanilla flavouring or being five acts long can be correct or mistaken, independently of whether people think they are or not.[14] This is a feature of our language, or, rather, of our language use; but that does not mean it is justified by the facts and should not be revised. If our application of literary appraisal terms is indeed partly grounded in our individual sense of satisfaction or dissatisfaction, then those terms are to that extent subjective. There is no question of the judgements employing them being correct or mistaken; a claim to universal validity is therefore unjustified and should be abandoned.

Another common objection to the kind of view proposed here is that if it were true, all literary judgements would be equally good; that is, would have equal standing. It might be said that the judgement that *King Lear* was bombastic, for instance, would, on this qualifiedly subjectivist account, be as good as the judgement that it was eloquent, and that the judgement that *King Lear* was bad was as good as the judgement that it was good. This is held to be an objection because it is supposed that one of those judgements – presumably the first in each case – is in fact manifestly wrong. Hume made a similar point; indeed, his celebrated essay *Of the Standard of Taste* is largely an attempt to reconcile the allegedly plausible commonsense view that some aesthetic judgements are clearly wrong with the apparently equally plausible commonsense view that beauty lies in the eye of the beholder.[15]

This objection is misplaced. In the first place, as we have seen, such judgements may, indeed, be faulty if they rely on nonaesthetic features of the thing judged or on inadequate perception of the relevant aesthetic features. But, setting that aside, the view relies on two questionable assumptions. The first is that most people entitled to make any judgement at all would in fact make the second judgement in each case about *King Lear* (that it was eloquent and good). But to assume that is to adopt a perilously parochial view, both temporally and locally. What we may now all judge eloquent or good other audiences in time or place may not. A case in point is Hume's own examples of the authors whose works he thinks it would be manifestly wrong to judge adversely. He mentions Homer and Virgil, certainly, whose reputations have possibly survived undimmed amongst the few who still read them. But he also mentions Addison and Terence, of whom not many of those few who still read them would now place equally in the first rank of literary authors. He regards it as self-evidently extravagant to regard Bunyan and Addison as equal in genius; but that is a judgement that few, perhaps, would support today. Indeed, the fact that those readers of both authors who were not already in the know would be hard pressed to say which one Hume regarded as clearly the inferior is evidence enough of the fragility of judgements he himself considered indubitable. It is questionable whether any author will stand the test of time (*all* human time?) and rash to suppose that because some have so far, they will continue to do so.

The second assumption, that those who do pass the test must be better than those who do not, or, in other words, that if, in fact, people's appraisals did agree over time, their verdict would be correct, is equally questionable.[16] That certain works did thus survive time's attritive passage, and that people did continue to agree in their estimation of them would by no means show, as we have pointed out, that their judgements were both objective and correct. It would show merely that, for whatever reason, people continued to find satisfaction in those works.

Does it matter?

Questions about the objectivity of aesthetic values can become heated, yet it does not seem that the answers matter very much – certainly not as much as the answers to corresponding questions about the objectivity of moral values, or the objectivity of scientific theories. The reason for this is connected with the purposes with which we read novels, look at pictures, listen to music, etc. In the case of literature, we seek various kinds of satisfaction – that of being involved in an interesting and moving, or subtle and amusing (the varieties are almost endless), make-believe world, for instance, or of experiencing an integration of sound, imagery, emotion and thought in a poem. Suppose, now, that objectivism were true, in the strong sense that every literary appraisal of the kind we have discussed were either correct or mistaken (remember that we are neglecting those – assuming there are some – which incorporate issues of truth). It would follow that if *King Lear* was moving, vivid, eloquent, etc., but I did not find it so, I would be mistaken, and I would be mistaken, too, if I found the play moving, vivid, eloquent, etc., although in fact it was not. How important would it be for me to be correct? Why should I care?

Well, suppose, first, that my judgement that the play was good in one or all of these ways was correct, but I felt no satisfaction in watching or reading it. This is certainly possible, since being right, on this account (though not on Kant's) does not entail being satisfied. Then being correct in my judgement would be scant consolation for having no satisfaction in watching or reading it. Now suppose my judgement of it was mistaken, but I felt a great deal of satisfaction in watching or reading it. This, too, is certainly possible, since being mistaken does not entail being dissatisfied. Then, too, being mistaken in my judgement would be of little consequence. For the aim of watching or reading the play is not to form a correct judgement of its value, but to enjoy it, to experience certain kinds of satisfaction in reading or watching it. If I fail to get those kinds of satisfaction, being correct in my judgement will be small compensation, and if I do, being mistaken in my judgement will scarcely disturb me.

Contrast this with moral or scientific judgements. It matters quite a lot whether we are mistaken or not about the laws of gravity, or the stress tolerance of the metal in a bridge, or about the rightness or wrongness of euthanasia. For our aim in undertaking scientific or moral inquiries is to reach the truth about some matter, or to make something work effectively, or to act rightly. Hence being mistaken about these things can have direct and momentous consequences. Being mistaken or not about the goodness of a play or a poem (assuming for the sake of argument, as we presently are, that, irrelevant or inadequately grounded judgements being set aside, it is possible to be so) would not have momentous consequences. For our aim in reading a play or a poem is neither directly cognitive (to find out what its value is) nor directly practical (to get something fixed or do what is right), but to obtain varied and complex kinds of satisfactions. Hence, even if we thought that objectivism was true, 'X is a poor novel, but I enjoy reading it', would normally cite an adequate reason for reading X, whereas 'P is false, but I enjoy believing it', would not normally cite an adequate reason for believing P, and 'Y is morally wrong, but I enjoy doing it', would not normally cite an adequate reason for doing Y.

Conclusion

We started by distinguishing three positions, objectivism, relativism and subjectivism. Our discussion has suggested that relativism stands very little chance of being true, and that the terms we use for literary appraisal generally, though probably not universally, have both an objective and a subjective element. Beauty seems to lie partly at least in the eye of the beholder. We have also seen that, since we read literature to obtain certain kinds of satisfaction, not to arrive at a true judgement of its value, disputes about the objectivity or otherwise of literary appraisals are less important than they may seem. But discovering why that is so yields insights into the nature of the appreciation of literature that we might not otherwise have obtained and which it was worth our while to discover.

NOTES

1 WHAT IS LITERATURE? CLEARING THE GROUND

1 *Lyra Graeca*, J. M. Edmonds (ed.), Harvard University Press, 1964, II, p. 352 (my translation). According to Herodotus (*History*, Book VII, 228), this inscription was placed over the graves of the Spartans (Lacedaemonians) who died defending the pass at Thermopylae against the invading Persian army in 490 BC.

2 Philosophers commonly invoke what is known as the type-token distinction in discussing these matters. But this distinction is easier to invoke than to explain. Thus I can point out that there are three occurrences of the letter 'p' in the first sentence of this note. It seems easy to reformulate that remark as 'There are three *tokens* of the *type* 'p' in that sentence. Armed with this shiny terminology, we could go on to say that the particular sound- and inscription-sequences, or the sentences uttered on particular occasions, are tokens, while the sequences, or sentences of which those particular utterings are utterings, are types; or that copies of discourses are tokens and the discourses of which they are copies are types. So far, so good. But anyone who tries now to explain the distinction further, particularly to an audience unfamiliar with it, will, I think, be compelled to recognise that it is far from clear. For we are talking about types without knowing what they are. The terminology thus seems to promise an enlightenment which in the end it does not deliver. (An example of this is, I suspect, provided by Richard Wollheim's attempt to explain the distinction in his *Art and its Objects*, Penguin, Harmondsworth, 1970, sections 35–37. While Wollheim succeeds in distinguishing neatly between types and universals (see below), he is not so successful in clarifying the ontological status of types. But if that is not clarified, nothing can be really clear.) In this way the distinction resembles that between universal and instance (this white page that you are now reading being said to be an 'instance' of the 'universal' whiteness, of which the succeeding page is a further 'instance') – another pair of terms it is seductively easy to use, but hard to explain. The trouble in both cases is that the senior partner of the pair (type, universal) is ontologically suspect – or at least opaque. Hence the illusion of enlightenment is bought at the cost of real obscurity further down the road. By resisting the allure of the type-token distinction, I have tried to avoid at least that obscurity.

3 It was first published in parts over a period of two years.

2 WHAT IS LITERATURE? DEFINITIONS AND RESEMBLANCES

1 For a detailed discussion of attempts to define art (not merely literature), see Stephen Davies, *Definitions of Art*, Cornell University Press, Ithaca/London, 1991. Davies reaches somewhat different conclusions about art in general from those I reach about literature in particular. See n. 24.

2 See L. Wittgenstein, *Philosophical Investigations*, tr. G. E. M. Anscombe, Blackwell, Oxford, 1953, pt I, sections 65 ff.

3 Wittgenstein, ibid., s. 66: 'Don't say "There *must* be something common..." but look and see whether there is anything common to all ... To repeat: don't think, but look!'

4 See, e.g., R. Wellek, *A History of Modern Criticism*, Yale University Press, New Haven, 1991, vol. 7, pts II and III; P. Steiner, *Russian Formalism: A Metapoetics*, Cornell University Press, Ithaca/London, 1984, chs 1 and 2; D. W. Fokkema and Elrud Ibsch, *Theories of Literature in the Twentieth Century*, C. Hurst, London, 1978, ch. 2.

5 *Collected Poems*, Jonathan Cape, London, 1943, pp. 140–1:

> What is this life, if, full of care,
> We have no time to stand and stare.
>
> No time to stand beneath the boughs
> And stare as long as sheep or cows...

6 See R. E. Scholes, *Structuralism in Literature*, Yale University Press, New Haven, 1974), p. 11: 'In particular, structuralism seeks to explore the relationship between the system of literature and the culture of which it is a part'. This work does not attempt a definition of literature, although a 'definition of fiction' is alluded to, but not formulated, in the discussion of Genette on p. 164 ff.

7 T. Todorov, 'Language and Literature', in Richard Macksey and Eugenio Donato (eds), *The Structuralist Controversy: The Language of Criticism and the Sciences of Man*, Johns Hopkins University Press, Baltimore, 1972, p. 130: 'While in speech the integration of units does not go beyond the level of the sentence, in literature sentences are integrated again as parts of larger articulations (*énonces*), and the latter in their turn into units of greater dimension, and so on until we have the entire work'.

8 See 'To Write: An Intransitive Verb?', in Macksey and Donato, op. cit., p. 136: 'The structure of the sentence is found again, homologically, in the structure of works. Discourse is not simply an adding together of sentences, it is, itself, one great sentence'. This claim has been criticised effectively by S. H. Olsen in *The Structure of Literary Understanding*, Cambridge University Press, Cambridge, 1978, pp. 17–18.

9 Jonathan Culler, *Structuralist Poetics*, Routledge & Kegan Paul, London, 1975, p. 129.

10 See Werner Bauer et al., *Text und Rezeption: Wirkungsanalyse zeitgenössicher Lyrik am Beispiel des Gedichtes 'Fadensonne' von Paul Celan*, Konstanz Univeritätsverlag, Frankfurt, 1972, p. 12. See also W. Iser, *Die Appellstruktur der Texte: Unbestimmtheit als Wirkungsbedingung Literarischer Prosa*, Konstanz Universitätsverlag, Frankfurt, 1970.

11 See 'The Concept of Literature', in *Literary Theory and Structure*, Brady, Palmer and Price (eds), Yale University Press, New Haven/London, 1978, pp. 23–39.

12 The primary source for speech act theory is J. L. Austin *How To Do Things With Words*, J. O. Urmson (ed.), Clarendon Press, Oxford, 1962. See also J. R. Searle, *Speech Acts: An Essay on the Philosophy of Language*, Clarendon Press, Oxford, 1969.

13 See 'Speech Acts and the Definition of Literature', in *Philosophy and Rhetoric*, 4, 1971, pp. 1–19. See also the same author's 'Speech, Literature and the Space Between', in *New Literary History*, iv, 1972–3, pp. 47–63. For a recent attempt (among several others) to connect speech act theory with literary theory (in this case, Deconstructionism), see S. Petrey, *Speech Acts and Literary Theory*, Routledge, London, 1990.

14 *The Collected Works of Elizabeth Barrett Browning*, intr. Karen Hill, Wordsworth, Ware, 1994, p. 327.

15 Sonnets XII, XVI and XVII. A number of Milton's sonnets are explicitly addressed to actual people, such as Cromwell and Lord Fairfax, although it is not of course always clear whether they were ever delivered to or, for that matter, read by them. Many other poets (Donne, for instance) have written verse letters to contemporary acquaintances.

16 Beardsley, op. cit., p. 34.

17 Beardsley, ibid., pp. 27, 37, 38.

18 Beardsley, *Aesthetics: Problems in the Philosophy of Criticism*, Harcourt, Brace and Wild, New York, 1958, pp. 122–6.

19 For Larkin, see his *The Less Deceived*, Marvell Press, Hessle, 1955, p. 16.

> No, I have never found
> the place where I could say
> This is my proper ground,
> here I shall stay...

For Laing, see his *Knots*, Tavistock Publications, London, 1970, p. 85:

> Before one goes through the gate,
> one may not be aware there is a gate to go through
> and look a long time for it
> without finding it...

There are of course more banal examples, including Dr Johnson's parody (Samuel Johnson, *Selected Writings*, Patrick Crutwell (ed.), Penguin, Harmondsworth, 1968, p. 501):

> I put my hat upon my head
> And walk'd into the Strand,
> And there I met another man
> Whose hat was in his hand.

Some of the criticisms I have made in this section have been forcefully put by C. A. Lyas, in 'The Semantic Definition of Literature', *Journal of Philosophy*, 66, 1969, p. 90.

20 See 'Defining Art', *American Philosophical Quarterly*, 6, 43, July, 1969, pp. 253–6. See also Dickie's *Art and the Aesthetic: An Institutional Analysis*, Cornell University Press, Ithaca, 1975; also his *Aesthetics: An Introduction*, St Martin's Press, New York, 1977.

21 'Defining Art', p. 255.
22 See S. H. Olsen, 'Literary Aesthetics and Literary Practice', *Mind*, 1981, vol. 90, p. 533; also his *The Structure of Literary Understanding*, Cambridge University Press, Cambridge, 1978, chs 4 and 5, and *The End of Literary Theory*, Cambridge University Press, Cambridge, 1987, pp. 73–87. Substantially the same view is advanced by Peter Lamarque and Stein Haugom Olsen in *Truth, Fiction and Literature*, Oxford University Press, Oxford, 1994, ch.10.
23 See 'The Notion Of Literature', in *New Literary History*, 5, 1973, p. 16: 'What the theoreticians have failed to do ... is to indicate the "specific difference" which characterises literature within the "genus proximum". Could it be that no such difference is in any way perceptible? In other words, that literature does not exist?'
24 For a discussion of family resemblance accounts of art, see Davies, op. cit., ch. 1. Davies thinks such accounts are questionable, although he does not specifically consider the case of literature.

3 FICTION

1 *Mimesis as Make-Believe: On the Foundations of the Representational Arts*, Harvard University Press, Cambridge, Mass./London, 1990, p. 35. A detailed and insightful account of literary fiction is given in Peter Lamarque and Stein Haugom Olsen, *Truth, Fiction and Literature*, Oxford University Press, 1994, chs. 2–3. My own account, however, while it in some ways resembles, does not coincide with theirs. See also Peter Lamarque, *Fictional Points of View*, Cornell University Press, Ithaca/London, 1996.
2 'Logical Status of Fictional Discourse', *New Literary History*, 6, 2, 1974–5, pp. 319–32. Searle's theory has been criticised by Gregory Currie (see n. 7) and by Lamarque and Olsen (see n.1).
3 Act III, Scene ii.
4 'Irony and the use-mention distinction', in P. Cole, (ed.) *Radical Pragmatics*, Academic Press, New York, 1981, pp. 295–318. A more recent version of their theory appears in the same authors' *Relevance: Communication and Cognition*, Oxford, 1986, ch. 4, section 9. The notion of interpretation is substituted there for that of mention in the earlier work. This leaves the theory equally vulnerable to the objection I raise against the original, and more detailed, version which I discuss in the text. For both versions maintain that the ironist echoes some believed proposition, thought or previously uttered remark. This seems to me not to be the case. Sperber has defended his views against a 'pretence' theory somewhat different from the one I give here, in 'Verbal irony: pretense or echoic mention?', *Journal of Experimental Psychology: General*, 113. 1, pp. 130–6 (see also pp. 112–29). The view he opposes is that of Clark and Gerrig (see n. 6, below). See also *Relevance and Communication*, p. 263, n. 25.
5 *Julius Caesar*, Act III, Scene ii.
6 That pretence has something to do with irony is an ancient view. It has been suggested more recently by H. P. Grice in 'Further notes on logic and conversation' in P. Cole, (ed.) *Syntax and Semantics: vol. 9, Pragmatics*, pp. 113–128; a more detailed account has been given by H. H. Clark and R. J. Gerrig in 'On the pretense theory of irony', *Journal of Experimental Psychology, General*, 113, pp. 121–6. My own view does not coincide exactly with that of any of these authors.
7 G. Currie, 'What Is Fiction?', *Journal of Art and Aesthetic Criticism*, XLIII, 4, 1984–5, pp. 385–92. A slightly revised version is in his *The Nature of Fiction*, Cambridge University Press, 1990, ch. 1. Currie prefers 'make-believe' to

'pretence', but he allows there is a use of 'pretence' which is synonymous with 'make-believe' and it is this use that I intend here – that of pretending to oneself – though I am not sure whether Searle has clearly distinguished it from other uses in his own analysis. See Currie, *The Nature of Fiction*, ch. 1, section 11; Searle, op. cit., passim.

8 This claim seems to have been dropped in *The Nature of Fiction*.

9 Caldar and Boyars, London, 1968.

10 p. 16.

11 Penguin, Harmondsworth, 1959.

12 'Homo sum; humani nil a me alienum puto.' *The Self-Tormentor*, 1, 1, 25.

13 There is controversy over whether we should speak of sentences or of propositions being true. For present purposes it does not matter which we do, since the point can be made using either locution. This does not mean, however, that the debate is a merely terminological one.

14 This is the conclusion reached by Currie in 'What Is Fiction?', p. 389 and in *The Nature of Fiction*, pp. 45–6.

15 *Truth, Fiction and Literature*, pp. 50–2.

16 Some of these issues are canvassed in *Truth, Fiction and Literature*, ch. 5.

4 PSYCHOLOGICAL REACTIONS TO FICTION

1 'Fearing Fictions', *Journal of Philosophy*, 75, (1978), pp. 5–27. See also *Mimesis as Make-Believe: On the Foundations of the Representational Arts*, Harvard University Press, Cambridge, Mass./London, 1990, ch.7. There has been considerable discussion of this topic in philosophical journals over the past twenty years. Of more recent works, see Bijoy H. Boruah, *Fiction and Emotion*, Oxford University Press, Oxford, 1988, an extensive treatment; Malcolm Budd, *Values of Art*, Penguin, London, 1995, pp. 110–123; Peter Lamarque and Stein Haugom Olsen, *Fiction, Truth and Literature*, Oxford University Press, Oxford, 1993, pp. 103–6.

2 But do I not feel fear for Anna as I read of her approaching the train, even though I am reading about her in the past tense?

3 See Colin Radford, 'How Can We Be Moved By The Fate Of Anna Karenina?', *Proceedings of the Aristotelian Society*, Supplementary Vol. 69, 1975, pp. 67–80.

4 See Michael Weston, ibid., pp. 81–93.

5 See *Biographia Literaria*, ed. J. Shawcross, Oxford University Press, Oxford, 1907, II, p. 6.

6 In his *Nicomachean Ethics*, VII, 2–4.

7 Walton holds that the person who has an irrational fear of flying does believe he is in danger, for he has both an 'intellectual' belief that he is not and a 'gut' belief that he is (*Fearing Fictions*, p. 8). But, considering that such people commonly say that they do not, or not really, believe they are in danger, it seems to beg the question simply to declare that the person has a belief that he is in danger, whether or not it is a 'gut' or some other kind of belief. Nor is it clear what a 'gut' belief is – he is simply afraid although he believes he is not in danger. If anything is in the gut, it is the fear, not the belief.

8 Corgi Books, London, 1970.

9 In his *Poetics*, VI, 1449b24–8.

10 Ibid. Cp. his *Politics*, VIII, 7. It is uncertain whether Aristotle understood 'purging' or 'purifying' by 'catharsis'. Some scholars consider the *Politics* passage explicates the *Poetics* passage, but Aristotle does not himself relate the two. In any case, the interpretation of both passages is obscure and controversial.

5 IMAGINATION

1 It was Gilbert Ryle who first suggested this, in recent times, in *The Concept of Mind*, Hutchinson, London, 1949, ch. 8. However, his account is a behaviourist one which I think is mistaken.

2 *Anna Karenina*, tr. Louise and Aylmer Maude, Oxford University Press, London, 1951, p. 380.

3 p. 394.

4 Roger Scruton, *Art and Imagination: A Study in the Philosophy of Mind*, Methuen, London, 1974, pp. 97–8.

5 'Imagine', like any other word, can of course be used ironically. If Tim had answered 'Well I'm at home and I'm looking at her, so I imagine she is,' he would not have been acknowledging the possibility of error, but speaking ironically. This can be explained in terms of the account of irony given in Chapter 3.

6 *Mimesis as Make-Believe: On the Foundations of the Representational Arts*, Harvard University Press, Cambridge Mass./London, 1990, p. 13.

7 Ibid.

8 I have argued this more fully in 'Walton on Imagination, Belief and Fiction', *British Journal of Aesthetics*, 36, 2, 1996, pp. 159–65.

9 Amos Oz, *Elsewhere, Perhaps*, Penguin, Harmondsworth, 1979, p. 180.

10 Act V, Scene i.

11 Op. cit., pp. 38–43.

6 METAPHOR

1 The philosophical literature on metaphor is vast. Three recent books which survey much of the previous discussion in the course of their own are Robert J. Fogelin, *Figuratively Speaking*, Yale University Press, New Haven, 1981, David Cooper, *Metaphor*, Oxford University Press, Oxford, 1986, and Eva Feder Kittay, *Metaphor*, Oxford University Press, Oxford, 1987. Anne Sheppard, *Aesthetics: An introduction to the philosophy of art*, Oxford University Press, Oxford, 1987, ch. 8 contains a brief discussion, while Peter Lamarque and Stein Haugom Olsen's *Truth, Fiction and Literature*, Oxford University Press, 1994, ch. 14, also offers a succinct treatment of the subject, particularly the topic of metaphorical truth.

2 See Max Black, 'Metaphor', *Proceedings of the Aristotelian Society*, 55, 1954, pp. 273–94. A slightly revised version, 'More About Metaphor', appears in A. Ortony, (ed.), *Metaphor and Thought*, Cambridge University Press, 1979, pp. 20–43. Black's views are partly supported in Kittay's *Metaphor* (see n. 1).

3 J. R. Searle, 'Metaphor', in *Metaphor and Thought* (see n. 2), pp. 92–123.

4 'What Metaphors Mean', *Critical Inquiry*, 5, 1978, pp. 31–47; repr. in *Inquiries into Truth and Interpretation*, Oxford University Press, Oxford, 1984, pp. 245–64. (References will be made to this volume.) This has been an influential paper. (A similar view was independently put forward by F. C. T. Moore in 'On Taking Metaphor Literally', in David S. Miall, (ed.), *Metaphor: Problems and Perspectives*, Harvester Press, Brighton, 1982, pp. 1–13. See also Stein Haugom Olsen's 'Understanding Literary Metaphors', in the same volume, pp. 36–54.)

5 p. 263.

6 'Howl', *Collected Poems 1947–95*, Penguin, London, 1996, p. 49.

7 Nelson Goodman, *Languages of Art*, Oxford University Press, London, 1969, pp. 77–8.

8 Both quotations are from *Collected Poems*, J. M. Dent & Sons Ltd., London, 1952. The first is from 'Once it was the Colour of Saying' (p. 89), the second from 'A Grief Ago' (p. 55).
9 Davidson, op. cit., p. 263.

7 INTERPRETATION AND INTENTION

1 See, e.g. Jacques Derrida, 'Limited Inc.', *Glyph*, 2, 1977, pp. 162–254, esp. pp. 179–80.
2 Useful comments on this much-discussed topic are in D. Newton-De Molina (ed.), *On Literary Intention*, Edinburgh University Press, Edinburgh, 1976, Anne Sheppard, *Aesthetics: An Introduction to the Philosophy of Art*, Oxford University Press, Oxford, 1987, ch. 7 and Stephen Davies, *Definitions of Art*, Cornell University Press, Ithaca/London, 1991, ch. 8.
3 Act I, Scene ii.
4 The principle does not, of course, license changes to the text which are not backed by strong evidence that the author misexecuted his own intentions. This is usually very hard to get, and it is therefore questionable how often editors will be in a position to make changes to what the writer leaves them on the page. Danis Rose's new edition of James Joyce's *Ulysses*, (Penguin, London, 1997) raises this question in an acute form. See Sarah Lyall, 'The Real "Ulysses"? Yes, He Said It Was, Yes', *International Herald Tribune*, June 24, 1997, p. 20.
5 *John Donne, Dean of St Paul's: Complete Poetry and Selected Prose*, John Hayward (ed.) , Nonesuch Press, London, 1949, p. 36.
6 In J. Margolis (ed.), *Philosophy Looks at the Arts*, Scribner's, New York, 1962, pp. 91–104.
7 p. 97.
8 In (for instance) *Validity in Interpretation*, Yale University Press, New Haven/London, 1967.
9 A similar view has been advanced by Jack W. Meiland in 'The Meanings of the Text', *British Journal of Aesthetics*, 21, 3, 1981, pp. 195–203.
10 *Collected Poems 1909–1935*, Faber and Faber, London, 1936, p. 15.
11 *Complete Poetry and Selected Prose* (see n. 5), p. 4.
12 'The Intentional Fallacy', in *Philosophy Looks at The Arts* (see n. 6), p. 104.
13 '1887', *Collected Poems of A. E. Housman*, Jonathan Cape, London, 1939, p. 10.
14 See Anne Sheppard, *Aesthetics* (see n. 2), pp. 109–110.
15 See W. Empson, *Some Versions of Pastoral*, Chatto and Windus, London, 1935, p. 133. This is noted by Donald Davidson in 'What Metaphors Mean', *Inquiries into Truth and Interpretation*, Oxford University Press, Oxford, 1984, p. 252.

8 LITERATURE, TRUTH AND MORALITY

1 part VII, c. 21.
2 The notion of such implication was extensively discussed by H. P. Grice on various occasions. See e.g. his *Studies in the Ways of Words*, Harvard University Press, Cambridge Mass., 1989.

The question of truth in fiction is discussed in David Lewis, 'Truth in Fiction', *American Philosophical Quarterly*, 15, 1978, pp. 37–46 (a seminal paper). Among more recent discussions are Gregory Currie, *The Nature of Fiction*, Cambridge University Press, Cambridge, 1990, ch. 2; Alex Byrne, 'Truth In Fiction: The Story Continued', *Australasian Journal of Philosophy*, 71, 1, 1993, pp. 24–35; Peter Lamarque and Stein Haugom Olsen, *Truth, Fiction, and*

Literature, Oxford University Press, Oxford, 1994, pp. 89–101; Derek Matravers, 'Beliefs and Fictional Narrators', *Analysis*, 55, 2, 1995, pp. 121–2. My own views differ somewhat from those of most of these authors (See Christopher New, 'A Note On Truth And Fiction', *Journal of Aesthetics and Art Criticism*, 55, 4, 1997, pp. 421–3, and comments by Matravers and Currie, pp. 423–7).

3 Faber, London, 1955.

4 'Ode On A Grecian Urn', *Poetical Works of John Keats*, H. Buxton Forman (ed.), Oxford University Press, London, 1908, p. 234.

5 This debate was set off, in modern times at least, by Arnold Isenberg, 'The Problem of Belief', *Journal of Aesthetics and Art Criticism*, vol. 13, 1954–5, pp. 395–407, repr. in Cyril Barrett (ed.), *Collected Papers on Aesthetics*, Blackwell, Oxford, 1965. For enlightening, though widely varying, recent discussions on some of the issues taken up in the rest of this chapter, see Hilary Putnam, 'Literature, Science, and Reflection', *New Literary History*, 7, 1975–6, pp. 483–92, repr. in *Meaning and the Moral Sciences*, Routledge and Kegan Paul, London, 1978; Anne Sheppard, *Aesthetics: An Introduction to the Philosophy of Art*, Oxford University Press, Oxford, 1987, ch. 8; Martha Nussbaum, *Love's Knowledge: Essays on Philosophy and Literature*, Oxford University Press, Oxford, 1990, (especially 'Flawed Crystals: James's *The Golden Bowl* and Literature as Moral Philosophy' and '"Finely Aware and Richly Responsible" Literature and the Moral Imagination'); Lamarque and Olsen, *Truth, Fiction, And Literature* (see n. 2), Part 3 (which contains a detailed exposition of a 'no truth' theory); Malcolm Budd, *Values Of Art: Pictures, Poetry And Music*, Penguin, London, 1995), ch. III. My own conclusions on these topics does not coincide exactly with any of these authors'.

6 Ch. IX, 1451b5–9.

7 George Dickie, 'Evaluating Art', *British Journal of Aesthetics*, 85, 1, 1985, p. 8.

8 See *The Republic*, Books III, 392c6–403a; IV, 435a–445e and X, 595a–608b. Plato argues in general that 'imitative' art appeals to a 'part' of the mind that is not the highest, rational, part. (What 'imitative' art is, and what 'parts' of the mind are, are questions which remain to some extent controversial.) It therefore seems to him to be a kind of 'ruin', or destruction, of the audience's intellect (595b5).

9 Penguin, London, 1988.

10 Some of them are discussed in Anne Sheppard, *Aesthetics* (see n. 5), ch. 9.

11 Richard W. Miller, 'Truth In Beauty', *American Philosophical Quarterly*, 16, 4, 1979, p. 322.

9 LITERARY APPRAISALS

1 In 'The Function Of Criticism', *Criterion*, October 1923, repr. in *Selected Prose of T. S. Eliot*, Frank Kermode (ed.), Faber and Faber, London/Boston, 1975, p. 69. The contemporary critic's book was F. R. Leavis, *The Common Pursuit*, Chatto and Windus, London, 1952.

2 See, e.g., Terry Eagleton, *Literary Theory: An Introduction*, Oxford University Press, Oxford, 1983, p. 11: 'There is no such thing as a literary work which is valuable *in itself*.' Compare Tzvetan Todorov, 'All Against Humanity', *Times Literary Supplement*, 4 October 1985, p. 1093: [Deconstructionism holds the thesis that] 'as no discourse is exempt from contradiction, there is no reason to favour one kind above another, or to choose one value rather than another.' (This is a view that Todorov does not himself endorse.)

3 The topic of value is a large one, and the literature on it is equally so. Among recent works are Anne Sheppard: *Aesthetics: An Introduction to the Philosophy of*

Art, Oxford University Press, 1987, chs. 5 and 6; George Dickie, *Evaluating Art*, Temple University Press, Philadelphia, 1988; David Wiggins, 'A sensible subjectivism?', in *Needs, Values, Truth*, Blackwell, Oxford, 1991; Anthony Savile, *Kantian Aesthetics Pursued*, Edinburgh University Press, Edinburgh, 1993; Peter Lamarque and Stein Haugom Olsen, *Truth, Fiction, and Literature*, Oxford University Press, Oxford, 1994, ch. 17; and Malcolm Budd, *Values of Art: Pictures, Poetry and Music*, Penguin, 1995, ch. 1. Two notable and influential classic works are David Hume, 'Of The Standard Of Taste', in *Essays Moral, Political and Literary*, Oxford University Press, Oxford, 1963, and Immanuel Kant, *Critique of Judgment*, tr. J. H. Bernard (New York, 1951).

4 Some might welcome this. See Terry Eagleton, op. cit., p. 11: ' "Value" is a transitive term: it means whatever is valued by certain people in certain situations, according to particular criteria and in the light of given purposes'. Would Eagleton accept 'a certain person in a certain situation'? If so, he would have adopted the position I describe, and to which he seems in any case to be committed.

5 Kant, op. cit., *Analytic of the Beautiful*, pp. 37–77.

6 ibid., pp. 54–76; see also the Deduction Of [Pure] Aesthetical Judgments, in the *Analytic of the Sublime*, pp. 120–82.

7 p. 60: '[w]e can hardly say that the pleasantness of one colour or the tone of one musical instrument is judged preferable to that of another in the same way by everyone'. In the next paragraph Kant considers the idea that sensation of 'simple' colours, untroubled by any 'foreign sensation' might be 'pure', and hence belong 'merely to form', thus entitling a claim for the colour to be regarded as beautiful (ibid.). The passage is obscure, but in any case, it apparently allows that 'composite' colours could not have such a status. But the idea of a simple colour's, but not a composite one's, being beautiful seems as implausible as the idea of all colours' not being so.

8 Actually, following common eighteenth-century practice, he divides aesthetic judgements into two types, judgements of the beautiful and judgements of the sublime. To judgements of the sublime he gives a slightly different treatment, in the *Analytic of the Sublime* (pp. 82–120). But the point remains that he has little concern with the variety of judgements we make under each of these categories.

9 Act IV, Scene iii.

10 'Good' and 'bad' need not be wholly unspecific: to say that x is a good novel is to say that it is good as a novel; hence, if x lacks the features characteristic of novels (say, plot and characters), it can no more be either a good or a bad novel than a creature that does not live in water can be either a good or a bad fish.

11 Compare Frank Sibley in Frank Sibley and Michael Tanner, 'Objectivity and Aesthetics', *Proceedings of the Aristotelian Society* Supplementary Volume, 42, 1968, pp. 3–54. Sibley, however, would not agree with the view I adopt here.

12 Not that our taste in food or drink may not sometimes expose us – Mr Hurst, in Jane Austen's *Pride and Prejudice*, ch. 8, when he found Elizabeth 'to prefer a plain dish to a ragout, had nothing more to say to her' – but that it does not do so in the same way.

13 On the objectification of values, see J. L. Mackie, *Ethics: Inventing Right and Wrong*, Penguin, Harmondsworth, 1977, ch. 1, esp. pp. 42–6. Mackie deals principally with ethical values, but his arguments are, I think, stronger when adapted to aesthetic values, so that one might reject some of his views on ethical value while accepting them on aesthetic value.

14 We sometimes say 'It's nice, although I don't myself like it.' This is generally to acknowledge the presence of features usually found satisfying which on this

occasion however are not found to be so, or to indicate that while they are satisfying on this occasion, there are other features that are not satisfying (and which
may outweigh those that are).

15 pp. 226–30. (See n. 3.)

16 For an account of this view see Antony Savile, *The Test of Time: An Essay in
Philosophical Aesthetics*, Clarendon Press, Oxford, 1982.

BIBLIOGRAPHY

The following recent books are of general interest. Detailed references to some of these and to other works are contained in the notes to each chapter.

Budd, Malcolm (1995) *Values of Art: Pictures, Poetry and Music*, London: Penguin.
Currie, Gregory (1990) *The Nature of Fiction*, Cambridge: Cambridge University Press.
Dickie, George (1971) *Aesthetics: An Introduction*, Indianopolis: Pegasus.
Lamarque, Peter (ed.) (1983) *Philosophy and Fiction: Essays in Literary Aesthetics*, Aberdeen: Aberdeen University Press.
—— (1996) *Fictional Points of View*, Ithaca/London: Cornell University Press.
Lamarque, Peter and Stein Haugom Olsen (1994) *Truth, Fiction and Literature*, Oxford: Oxford University Press.
Nussbaum, Martha (1990) *Love's Knowledge: Essays on Philosophy and Literature*, Oxford: Oxford University Press.
Olsen, Stein Haugom (1985) *The Structure of Literary Understanding*, Cambridge: Cambridge University Press.
—— (1987) *The End of Literary Theory*, Cambridge: Cambridge University Press.
Scruton, Roger (1974) *Art and Imagination: A Study in the Philosophy of Mind*, London: Methuen.
Sheppard, Anne (1987) *Aesthetics: An Introduction to the Philosophy of Art*, Oxford: Oxford University Press.
Walton, Kendall (1990) *Mimesis as Make-Believe: On the Foundations of the Representational Arts*, Cambridge, Mass./London: Harvard University Press.
Wollheim, Richard (1970) *Art and its Objects*, Harmondsworth: Penguin.

INDEX

imagining 75–6; and irony 43; and
  metaphor 93
psychological reactions: 53–5, 57–8;
  without belief 59–61; and behaviour
  53, 63

rationality and reactions to fiction 64–8
relativism 124, 125–6
representation 39, 51–2
Rezeptionsaesthetik 24–5
rigidity and translation 16–17

Scruton, Roger, on imagination 71
Searle, J. R.: on fiction 40–2; on
  metaphor 87–9
seeing as 51–2
self-deception 60
similes 85–6, 91
speech acts, theory of 25–6, 94
Sperber, Dan, and Deirdre Wilson on
  irony 42
Spoonerisms 97–8
structuralism 23–4
subjectivism 124, 126, 130–3

suspension of disbelief 58–9

text, establishment of 97–9
Todorov, Tzetvan, on definition of
  literature 34
translation: 14; of literary works 17
type-token distinction 138

universal validity, claim of aesthetic
  judgments to 128–9, 133–4
universals 138
utterer's meaning 87–9

Walton, Kendall: on fiction 79; on
  imagining 72–3; on psychological
  reactions to fiction 55–9; on
  representation 39, 52
weakness of will *see akrasia*
Wimsatt, William K. Junior, and
  Monroe C. Beardsley, on the
  Intentional Fallacy 194–6, 203
Wittgenstein, Ludwig, on Family
  Resemblances 20